THE BRIAR CLIFF REVIEW

Volume 28 • 2016

S0-BAC-411

CONTENTS

The REVIEW STAFF

Editor
Tricia Currans-Sheehan

Assistant Editors
Nikki Howard
Maddi Underwood

Design Editor
Shannon Beller

Fiction Editors
Phil Hey
Matthew Pangborn

Poetry Editor
Jeanne Emmons

**Nonfiction Editors &
Siouxland Editors**
Ryan Allen
Paul Weber

Art Editor
Jeff Baldus

Assistant Editorial Staff
Megan Aschoff
Claire Dufur
Melanie Krieps Mergen
Andrea Lahowetz
Angelica Mercado
Amelia Skinner Saint

Assistant Copy Editors
Jillian Hofer
Jamie Jacobsen
Maritza Resendiz
Mackenzie Schindler
Lindsey Sorlie

Assistant Design Editors
Desi Beckmann
Lindsay Ferris

Marketing Director
Judy Thompson

Publisher
Briar Cliff University

Printer
Anderson Brothers

ABOUT OUR COVER

ReBeckett

Bob Allen
mixed media on canvas

The Artist:

This mixed media painting on stretched canvas is a vivisected portrait of Irish author Samuel Beckett. Completed in 2015, it is the third in a series of paintings about writers that I admire; others in the series include Bertolt Brecht and Virginia Woolf. Here our subject is waiting at the intersection of yesterday and I don't remember.

In Barcelona

Graceann Warn
oil and encaustic on canvas

Thirty and Out

S.J. MacLean

Well of course people will cast blame. It's human nature to look for wrongdoing in others, and in those days, 1944 if memory serves right, there were plenty of reasons to accuse others of treason. Accidents happen, though, and individuals whose recollections have dulled have a way of forgetting, even those who believe they've been wronged. Ella bends over her journal and writes. *The coloreds were sent off to prison. The Japanese were sent off to the camps.* It's a shame things like that occurred, but people thought differently during the war, and who's to say which neighbors were so virtuous they would not have turned on each other?

Detroit's old Kelsey-Hayes plant, which faces her kitchen window, shadows the table where she writes. Bearing down on the number-two pencil she's worn to a stub, she'd like to get this out before four o'clock closes in on December's last day. Sharpening the pencil on a sharpener attached to the table, she starts again. A week before the Port Chicago explosion, Umeko and Takeshi Matsumoto with their three girls and two suitcases sat on the sidewalk in front of their house. Waiting for a bus to transport them to Tulelake, they turned away from her as she stood in the front window of her living room next door although she hadn't parted the curtains to gawk at her neighbors. It was James Jackson she was watching, walking the path to her house.

He didn't acknowledge her when Arthur opened the door; in those days whites and blacks didn't mingle and men in the services didn't mix, it being the war when people didn't mind what color got killed unless it was one of their own. He handed a document to Arthur. He was a Navy man, too.

"They want to interview you," said Arthur, after James left.

"I don't know why they'd want me."

"I suppose because you were home that day."

"Well that's true." Smoking a Chesterfield, she blew smoke in front of her face.

Thirty years retired and thirty years Arthur dead, and her only child, Sarah, twenty-four years gone. You never expect your child to pass before you do, even if she was sixty-two years old, but then, you don't expect your long-lost grandson to come around either. Though he hasn't yet shown up tonight. Don't tell her she's got to stuff her puffy feet into her shoes, pull up her black rubber boots, and slog through the snow. She'll have to melt the car lock with her lighter since she's not left the house in days, hope the car starts, and drive over to Vernor. It's New Year's Eve and she's got to retrieve Akin.

The war-like names parents give their kids these days, Akin, Alex, as if they want their little cretins to become warriors. People have no idea what a big war is like — not even, God forgive her the heresy — Vietnam. In forty-four everyone contributed; she certainly did. She loved the giant furnaces lapping up iron ore with their tongues at the foundry, men pouring the fiery molten waste into pots the size of small cars and outsized erector-set cranes stalking the Richmond docks. She even liked the sound of rivets going in from guns at the Ford plant. Ella stops writing and curls her right index finger. *Rat-a-tat tat, rat-a-tat tat*, a sound she likened to machine gun fire though the women making Jeeps thought it sounded more like laying down large carpet tacks.

Most of all she loved the lacey white veils showering her with fire when she welded and giant slabs of iron slamming down on the big ships. *BAM!* She pounds the kitchen table with a fist. *BAM! BAM!* Like that.

Everything was white light and important, full of big noise.

Oh yes, she was someone during the war, building the big Boulder Class Victory ships in Richmond, California. Then the war ended, she and Arthur returned home to Detroit, and soon she became one of those women people don't much talk about anymore.

She picks up her pencil and bears down so hard on the journal page, the pencil tip breaks.

Ten o'clock and Akin not here, she drives down Michigan Avenue and heads over to Vernor. She flicks on the wipers to clear snow from the windows. If the police stop her she'll put on her Alzheimer's act, the one she started using after the DMV took away her license for good. It makes her mad she can't recall the year it happened; she likes to think she's still sharp, although with snow and sleet sliding down the windshield, she has to admit her vision is shot. She'll write that down later and maybe even read it out loud when her senior journaling class gets back together again in two weeks. A certain amount of honesty is important. *The journal's about you*, the twenty-five-year old instructor, Felicia, who doesn't like that Ella writes in the third person, had said. *Couldn't you switch over?*

No she could not. The girl's clicking tongue studs were starting to annoy her.

Dusky violet clouds in a dead winter sky turn the bronze archways of Michigan Central Station slime green. Parking in front of the monstrosity, she lets the motor run and surveys broken glass in the old railroad station's entryway doors. There are no other cars on the street but she's not afraid, as most of her neighborhood in southwest Detroit, where she's lived on Gilbert Street for over forty-five years, is empty too. Of course if someone saw her parked in front of Michigan Central Station, the very same train depot to which she and Arthur returned from California after the war, they might think her memory is gone. Thank you very much, it is not.

> Since she's the only able-minded woman left in Detroit who built the big ships, she's been asked to give a little speech about what it was like in those days.

When Akin told her he'd found the barbed wire surrounding the building cut, she knew immediately he'd crawled through the wire, avoided broken glass in a window or one of the massive front doors, and gone in. Now, although he says he's just curious and denies it, she suspects he is living there.

"You should see the place, Nana. Blues and greens, reds, yellows and oranges on the columns and archways, everything so big and beautiful it's like an explosion."

For a moment she thought the colors he saw were residue from the brain injury he'd suffered in Iraq, until he mentioned the graffiti, but it wasn't so much the colors that tipped her off how the station seduced him, it was the way his face seemed to take on a glow. She knows the thrill. It's the power of destruction he loves, as if a bomb had rocked the great door and windows, archways and columns into a trashed wasteland. How is it that the explosion in Iraq leads him to darkness while the shock wave knocking her and James from bed those many years ago, followed by a fireball broiling the sky, forever set her aflame?

A half hour it's been, maybe she should crawl into the building, but it's probably better to let her grandson know she's not stalking him, so she waits until a group of men duck through holes in the glass of the station's front doors. As Akin ghosts toward her, she steps from the car.

"I thought you might need a ride."

He climbs in the front seat and they drive home to Gilbert Street.

About two months ago her grandson shocked her when he showed up at her door. His mother had moved to Oakland, California when he was around two years old, one of the reasons she and her daughter had become so estranged. Sarah had wanted nothing to do with the city that every day reminded her of the father she never knew. "You're my only family, Nana," Akin said. "I want to be here for you." It was soon obvious, though, she needed to be here for him, a thirty-one-year-old man with no job. Refusing to stay with her, he told her he was living with friends.

Ella pours hot water from a kettle over her Sanka and carries her coffee cup and a bottle of beer to the kitchen table.

"I'm not supposed to drink, Nana."

"You stay in that train station you'll be drinking."

"It's the medicine."

"New Year's Eve, one's not going to hurt. I want you to come with me to the veterans' ceremony next week. If you show pride in your service and reconnect with the military, it will help you get back to normal."

You would think she had asked him to eat lunch with the Devil. He's ashamed to attend the city-sponsored celebration for war veterans on Belle Isle, with a special dedication to women who supported the troops during World War II. Since she's the only able-minded woman left in Detroit who built the big ships, she's been asked to give a little speech about what it was like in those days. What an honor.

"I can't, Nana. People still talk."

They do, particularly about men who walk away from war. She'd seen the newspaper accounts how members of his platoon had accused him of deserting after an explosion. They say he'd disappeared and Iraqi police found him days later wandering along a dry river bed. Although nothing came of an inquiry, and a doctor testified men who appear uninjured often suffer brain injuries from explosion shock waves, rumors keep circling. Well she knows something about rumors, how they feed on themselves.

Ella slices air with the sharp-boned edge of one hand. "The truth will come out."

That's what James Jackson said, after the Navy inquiry began. The look on his face, she'll never forget it, and to this day she doesn't know whether it was sheer hatred or something worse, a statement of fact. "Sooner or later the truth will come out, Ella. It always does." About ten years ago she thought she saw him in the post office on Springwells Street when a man in front of the line, next to the counter, held her gaze steady, and even then, some fifty plus years later, she turned away. When he walked past her, though, he was just another old man.

"The military was my life," Akin says. "I'm washed up. It's wrong."

"Wrong? You should know wrong."

After she and Arthur came home to Detroit, the factories wouldn't hire women welders, and she was supposed to stay home and feed her baby out of a bottle. Arthur was a good man and they'd had a good marriage; he accepted the child. Eventually she found work on the line at Fleetwood although it wasn't what she wanted. She wanted slabs of metal, steel beams, blast furnaces, and fire. Even Arthur, after thirty years on the line at Jefferson Assembly, didn't realize how useless he would become after retiring, but that's how it was in those days. Thirty years working, guaranteed out, the union had fought long and hard for the right to become nothing, and within a month after retiring he died of a heart attack. It amazes her that she herself is thirty years past retirement when it was a running joke among auto workers that after you retired you would drop dead the next day.

"When the war ended," she says, "everything changed suddenly. Like that!" She puts down her coffee cup and stops. Her grandson is staring at her. Coffee has spilled onto her hand and there's a chip on the bottom rim of her good china cup.

Cracks and booms everywhere, she shuffles to a front window to look out. It's midnight and her neighbors, whoever's left of them, are standing on the sidewalk shooting guns at the stars. Cherry bombs explode and rockets pierce holes in the curtain of night. She turns to wish Akin Happy New Year but the front door's wide open and her grandson's not there. Walking outside as quickly as her left hip will allow, she finds him standing on the sidewalk mesmerized by the fireworks, and when she reaches him he's clutching at the ends of his red flannel shirt, which is hanging out of his pants. He is weeping.

"Oh no, Akin, dear boy, everything will be all right."

When the neighborhood finally quiets and her grandson falls asleep in the second bedroom down the hall, she returns to her journal and flips open the gray cover to the first page. What did the class hope to achieve by keeping a journal, Felicia had asked her students. Write it down. But Ella could think of only two items: (a) explain what happened and (b) make things right. Lately she's started to see her days living in Port Chicago and working in Richmond in color, rather than in black and white, and last week in the Senior Center, while passing the open door of an art room on her way to her journaling class, a brown swirl on white canvas startled her. She saw James' hand on her skin.

What a time they'd had in an underground club over in Vallejo where there were other mixed couples, dancing, drinking, listening to music, always careful to avoid acknowledging each other if they happened to pass on Richmond's bustling streets. If she was with Arthur, who knew James only because he'd recognized him as one of the

mechanics in a Detroit garage where he took his car, and acknowledged him with a tilt of his head, or maybe a few words, she nodded, too. But that was about it.

Glancing through the window at the darkened Kelsey-Hayes plant, which the city is planning to demolish, she concentrates. Amazing how buildings, people, and even history change. How, depending upon your vantage point, the past is never still and memory is slippery and adjusts to the person you want to be. She'd been thinking about that for some time and after Akin arrived in Detroit, she acted and willed him the house. It's not worth much, but he can live in it or sell it to pay medical people to do whatever it is they do for traumatized people these days. Money, though, that comes and goes. Money is never enough. She doesn't know for sure her grandson didn't desert and imagines she never will, but one thing she will leave him is the certainty that James Jackson was right.

A hand on her thigh, a roar, the sky is on fire. Shredded curtains sway wildly, windows shatter, and Arthur's Navy black dress shoes glow orange. A second boom and she flies from bed, hits the wall, and falls to the floor. Pinned by a toppled dresser her ears hum, smoke and flame build massive columns in the night sky and Japanese warplanes fly through her fear. White light, screaming, the world is imploding, and yet she feels light. The weight on her legs disappears. Is Arthur pushing the bureau away? Oh yes, that's right, Arthur's on duty tonight. James searches her face with his fingers, lifts her from the floor and clings to her as they stumble past shards of glass to the front door. They jump off the porch, which no longer has steps. A mound of boards that used to be the porch of Umeko and Takeshi's bungalow rests on the ground, chimney bricks trail down the sloped roof, and Helen Richardson, who lives across the street, next to the Wilsons, appears in the doorframe of her house, which is missing the roof. Making their way along the street with a few of her neighbors — she can no longer recall who — they pass two upended car frames so twisted it's impossible to determine the make, pieces of metal from baby carriages and children's trikes, and splintered piles of wood that used to be houses.

"The ships," people are shouting.

Almost everyone's heading toward the port but smoke billows everywhere, occluding the sky, and forces them back as ghastly, orange clouds spirit through haze and fire in the distance, narrowing a slit between daylight and night.

"Where's the post office?" someone says. "Wasn't it over there?"

At one-thirty in the morning, it's a new year. A good time to reconcile an accounting of the disaster, to square up facts that have accumulated in her mind, particularly since she stopped working thirty years ago. To this day she wonders if she imagined what she witnessed or whether she created details that magnified the explosion to make it even more catastrophic than it was. As if such a thing were possible. Did she make up the fact that when she and James tried to reach the port a man stopped them and said *there ain't no port no more?* Or that one of the two ships men were loading with shells and bombs had been obliterated and the other had been blown out of the water?

It wouldn't have been possible to see those events, she later realized, since a firestorm was eating the sky and devouring structures and equipment that hadn't been annihilated. Especially the dead men, three hundred and twenty in all, many of their bodies were never found. And yet she's continued to embellish over the years, sometimes telling people over five hundred black men died or that close to a thousand people sustained injuries and she helped build one of the destroyed ships, the *S.S. E. A. Bryan*, when she hadn't.

It used to feel good to create facts about the explosion so devastating they would overwhelm crimes committed in the aftermath, make them shrink in comparison, seem small.

Ella resumes writing and considers what to include in the speech she plans to give Sunday, which she'll share with her journaling class. She will tell her audience it was considered a great honor to build liberty ships during the war while the men were off fighting, how after the war women were dismissed as if they were nothing, and what terrible injustices occurred such as sending the Matsumotos off to a camp and putting all those black men in jail.

When you think of it, which she does every day as she nears her end, the wrongs were enormous. It seemed to her within days of the explosion, even before all the body parts were located and the *Quinalt Victory* was discovered upside down in water five hundred yards away from the dock, rumors started. Enlisted men loading the ships with shells and bombs had sabotaged them, people said, and by the time the Navy Court of Inquiry began four days later, the rumors had fed on themselves and mushroomed. The enlisted laborers were of an inferior class. They had no experience handling live arms.

James was in the first group of men who refused to load ammunition onto a ship arriving at Mare Island three weeks later, and many of them were arrested. Although some of the surviving enlisted men had been evacuated to Camp Shoemaker in Oakland, he had been ordered to stay in Port Chicago to search for body parts. When he met her in a little motel next to the Horse Cow Bar in Vallejo, he seemed dazed.

"You've got to tell them, Ella," he said. "Tell them I was with you that night."

Shaken by the way his hands trembled and sweat dripped off his brow, she didn't respond. As perspiration dampened his heavy brows and made his skin glisten, he continually shifted toward a window and jumped when a door down the hall slammed. It wasn't so much how worried he was about being seen in the motel that rattled her as it was how fragmented he appeared, so pulled apart. He must have sensed how fearful she was about testifying, how the consequences might pull apart her own life, because that's when he told her, "Sooner or later the truth will come out, Ella. It always does."

She supposes her silence caused him doubt, just as some of her neighbors must have seen him on the walk to her house on those afternoons or nights when Arthur was working and never said anything. But someone betrayed her. After James was arrested, she heard people speculate how he was a leader in the mutiny because he wanted to sabotage the war effort and that's why he wasn't at the pier the night of the explosion. He was a deserter.

Years after the war she learned he did twelve years.

All of this Ella records. She writes compulsively as if her life depended upon the facts of who she once was and had strived to be and who she wants to become, which, when she considers herself at age eighteen and at the advanced age she is now, isn't all that much different. Finally, exhausted, at three-thirty in the morning she goes to bed, and when she wakes up, her grandson is gone.

> As perspiration dampened his heavy brows and made his skin glisten, he continually shifted toward a window and jumped when a door down the hall slammed.

When Akin doesn't visit her for five days, she toys with the idea of crawling through the hole in the barbed wire at the train station to confront him, yet hesitates and allows herself a glimmer of hope because not once before New Year's Eve had he slept at her house. She doesn't want to shock him although Sunday morning, surprise of surprises, Akin gives her a jolt. Banging the knocker on her door, the doorbell having given up close to fifteen years ago, he smiles at her nervously when she lets him inside.

"I won't go to the honoring ceremony, Nana, but I want you to know I'm proud of you."

This declaration of faith that should cause her joy, she's afraid she might cry. Her grandson leans over her. How much height has she lost over the years? Three inches? Four? She will not be diminished. Even after she dies she will not have anyone considering her small.

"I have important things to say. I want you to hear."

"No."

"Don't go to that train station anymore. I'm leaving you the house. When I'm gone – " he opens his mouth, but she silences him by raising a hand – "promise me you'll talk to medical people and stay here. And go through my papers. The deed and insurance documents are in the front of my journal. Promise you'll read it."

"I'm going to stay here tonight, Nana, but don't talk like that."

"Say it! You must say it!"

Her grandson looks slightly amused, and for some reason that gives her another small flicker of hope. "I do. I promise."

Using her good hip to hoist herself onto the middle rail, she leans forward. Staring downriver, the bridge lights come on, and so do the lights across the river in Windsor and at the Ren Cen and other skyscrapers.

Close to seventy people nod in solemn agreement when she tells them how women helped build the liberty ships in Richmond and how she lived in Port Chicago when the explosion destroyed so much. Not just the ships and port, nor the lives of men sent to prison, but something more important, the truth. Black enlisted men went to prison for mutiny while their white officers went free. Although the injustice of it all has long been acknowledged, she tells the audience, an assortment of veterans and government dignitaries, she's here to right wrongs. After her talk, people gather around tables to eat small cakes, puff pastries, and flakey-crust tartlets and drink tea and coffee as several people ask her questions and discuss their own service. Some even thank her.

When the sun dips low in the sky and casts orange light through the floor to ceiling windows, she leaves Flynn Pavilion and drives toward MacArthur Bridge, which spans the river from Belle Isle. When she reaches the bridge she stops, parks her car, gets out and walks to the rail to look at the city's skyline. Periodically turning toward her unlocked car, she doesn't want anyone stealing her purse on the front seat and tossing her identification, what's left of it, a library and medical insurance card, into a garbage bin. She will not be anonymous.

Using her good hip to hoist herself onto the middle rail, she leans forward. Staring downriver, the bridge lights come on, and so do the lights across the river in Windsor and at the Ren Cen and other skyscrapers. Sun slips down glass buildings, bronzes black water blue. She loves what this city once was. Zug Island blast furnaces throwing off flames, locomotives powering right into the factory at Rouge, and freighters carrying coke and iron ore pulling up to the docks. As silly as it sounds, she even liked the sight of Levy's old slag heap. Now look at the place. Three dollar cupcakes and five dollar coffee, for one cup, mind you, up near the university.

What a fine day this was. The audience was so appreciative and the elegant little pastries and flower arrangements on tables overlooking the river, something you might expect to find at classier gatherings. Sunlight poured through the windows the entire time she was there. Imagine! A sunny January day in Detroit although the temperature is frigid and ice flows drift on the river. Veterans and government officials will remember her, not that she told them everything, of course. She didn't mention, for example, the journal entry she wrote just this morning about the inquiry and the burdens some people carried years later.

And what would she have told them? That people were different during the war so wrongs were committed? You don't share a journal with strangers. Anyway, these days it's all public record, so if people want to know more about the explosion and its aftermath they can look it up on their computers or go to the library. Strangers don't need to know details that have stayed with her all these years, the questions the officer at the inquiry asked, and how she tilted toward him and focused on his medals to still her anxiety. The man's uniform was deep blue, his medals bright brass.

"Mr. Jackson claims he was with you."

"I can't help what he claims."

"He was not at your house that night?"

"No."

"Well, which is it? Was he there or was he not?"

"No Sir. He was not."

To this day she recalls how she tried to narrow the distance between her and the officer, as if by angling into him she could project confidence and weaken his doubts, and apparently it worked. People, when confronted with difficult choices, will rationalize the truth. Ella leans over the rail toward the Navy man, stretches toward bronze and blue, and as the sun falls away and the Detroit River blackens, she closes the distance between them, and the day's light goes out.

Spruce Island, ME, 2015

Ron Johns
photograph

Laura Apol

Midwinter, My Mother

After I left the cemetery, I drove –
east to the ocean, seven states away.
The journey was slow, weighted as I was,
myself in my arms. I thought

she would go with me. I thought
she would stay with me in my sleep. Instead,
I dreamed of fallen horses, ruins of battle.
– those useless limbs, those dying

horses' eyes. I walked on the beach
until I understood: how water and time
grind down the world, hand us our cartilage,
broken. Hand us our bones.

She'd known, in the end, because
I had to tell her. I stood by her bed,
kept my mind on the moon, the clear
winter light. I wanted

to hear her say she loved me,
and I pretended she did, pretended
I heard those words in the waves –
above shards of shell, fish bones picked clean.

#18

Rick Johns
acrylic and graphite on wood panel

On Kindness

Laura S. Distelheim

Black is how I remember it. The kind of black that won't meet your eyes. That looks away, unimpressed, no matter how fervently you beg it for mercy. Why I was there – alone in my stalled car, by the side of a road whose name I wasn't sure of – and where I was en route to or from, I've since forgotten. This was long ago. But the vacuum around me, the moonlessness and the mercilessness, the *hoos* and whistles and hisses and screeches of nocturnal secrets, and the terror, I remember. *That* I remember, and this: That, when my fingers finally managed to stutter out the number of my emergency roadside assistance service on my cell phone, the voice that bloomed on the other end of the line answered with, *Are you somewhere that you feel safe?* Not a question at all, but a life vest, and I slipped my arms into its kindness and buckled it around me and zipped it straight up to my chin.

I once dated a man whose father had warned him against being too kind for fear that it would make people perceive him as weak. I hated hearing that when he told it to me, less for what it said about him (because, despite his father's best efforts, he was, in fact, kind), than for what it said about kindness itself. I, for one, know that it gets a bad rap. Want me to show you? Come with me: Back to a morning just over a year ago, at a hospital fifty or so miles from my home, where I have gone to be subjected to a test I don't want to take, ordered by a doctor I don't want to know, for a chronic illness I don't want to have, that has cast me in a life story I don't want to be mine, all of which I have muttered and ranted about in perfect duet with Springsteen, set to full blare (*No retreat, baby, noooooooooooooooooo surrENder),* for nearly the entire hour and a half it has taken me to get here, my hands vised on the steering wheel as I centime-tered my way through a clot of city traffic (starting, stopping, starting, stopping, getting lost, retracing, starting, stopping) so that, by the time I pull up to its entrance, I'm dragging the full fury and frustration inflamed by decades of battles – of lying in antiseptic halls on pushed-to-the-side gurneys, waiting for radiology to call me in; of being the g.i.case / infectious disease case / ortho case / neurology case / rheumatology case / pre-op case / post-op case in room 512 /room 780 / room 432 / room 285; of wearing green gown after green gown after green gown that turned my face anonymous – behind me like a ruckus of tin cans that are clattering from my fender.

It's no wonder the valet parking attendant looks up, startled, when I stagger out of the driver's seat. "I have a handicapped placard," I tell him as I give him my keys, because that's what the sign on the wall behind him instructs me to do. If I have one. Which I do. Which I do and do and do. Which I DO. It isn't his fault. I know that *none* of this is his fault, but the words come out more like an accusation than an an-nouncement anyway, which may explain why he repeats them as a question; "You have a handicapped placard?"

He can see this any way he wants to. He can see this as a race thing, a class thing, a socioeconomic thing, a simple rudeness thing. But instead his voice is full of knowing exactly what that means – what the words mean and what the way I've said them means – and the look he gives me is a hand that I hold onto for the rest of the day. Weak? I don't think so. In fact, here it is, his gentle gesture, more than a full year later, still going strong.

Kindness has a way of doing that – of living on long past the culmination of its actual lifespan. And, unfortunately, lack of kindness shares the same skill. "What I regret most in my life are failures of kindness," the author, George Saunders, told the 2013 graduating class of Syracuse University when delivering its convocation speech and, hearing him repeat that statement in a recent television interview, I was immediately transported to a twilit moment nearly three decades ago on a sidewalk in Cambridge, Massachusetts, where I was a few months into my first year as a student at Harvard Law School.

This wasn't my first time as a first year grad student. Three years earlier, still reeling from my most recent ten rounds with my illness, I'd started as a student at another school, where it had felt, from the moment I set foot on its campus, as if I were wearing my life like a misbuttoned coat. No matter how much I yanked at its collar or tugged at its sleeves, that life continued to hang crooked from my shoulders, until finally, at the end of that year, I'd unbuttoned it, tore it off, and left it in a puddle behind me. So that when, two years of regathering strength and regaining direction later, I was accepted to HLS, it had felt less like I'd been invited back to grad school than that I'd been handed yet another life to try on, and I had started out the year there holding my breath, not daring to believe that it would fit me.

It did. Slipped onto my skin and fell into place around my bones as if it had been custom tailored for me, which is why, there I was, walking down the sidewalk at that twilit moment, surfing the crest of a wave of relief. And there, heading toward me, half a block or so away, was a classmate whom I'd never talked to but had seen across the room in several of my classes, unmistakably tugging at the sleeves and yanking at the collar of his own life. Something about the way his shoulders were hunched, about the way his hands were in his pockets, about the way his head was cocked and his smile was almost apologetic in the moment when our eyes met as we passed one another, gave me the impulse to reach out and touch his arm and ask if he wanted to stop in somewhere, maybe, have a cup of coffee maybe, and, you know, just talk. But I didn't because, well, I didn't.

> It isn't easy, kindness. You might even say that it can be perilous because, let's face it: It can backfire big time.

I didn't because I wasn't the kind of woman who did those types of things, who moved through the world with that kind of easy grace. I had always been the sick girl who was frequently missing long stretches of school and then returning on crutches or with a new set of scars or twenty pounds thinner. And even though I thought I had felt something – a sadness, a *please*, a *come get me* – when our eyes met as we passed each other at that moment, I hadn't trusted it. *What if I'm wrong?* or *What if he doesn't want to?* or *What if he thinks it's strange of me to ask?* is what I'd busied myself with thinking as I'd moved on past him on the sidewalk and so no, I hadn't trusted it.

Not at first, anyway. Not until the next day, when I'd finally gathered my courage and had gone to his dorm room and had found the door ajar and the room in-your-face empty. Not just empty, but emptied out. His closet door open, its hangers naked and askew, his bed stripped and his desktop swept clean, the chair – the chair where I had imagined I'd find him sitting, in all the scenarios I'd practiced in my head on my way over – set back at an angle, vacant. Dropped out, a guy who lived in a room across the hall told me when I knocked on his door to ask. Dropped out with no forwarding address.

It's still with me, that moment on the sidewalk when I passed him and didn't reach out. It's still with me all these years later, having trailed me through the decades of twilights that have bloomed and waned since that one. It doesn't come to me often, but there are still moments, maybe especially in winter if I'm walking down a sidewalk where the hills of snow that have been plowed up against the curb are soaking the dusk into their folds until they have blued, when I'll find myself imag-

ining for an instant that there he is, coming toward me, and knowing all over again that no, no he's not. That that chance to be kind is long past and I can never get it back. Can never do it over, do it right, reach out, touch his arm, say those words, let him know that he's not the only one.

So yes, I'm right there beside George Saunders in counting failures of kindness among my greatest regrets. Which is why I've done my best ever since that time to try to avoid them. But even as I have, I've understood the self who didn't stop on the sidewalk that day. It isn't easy, kindness. You might even say that it can be perilous because, let's face it: It can backfire big time. I've learned that lesson the hard way, too. A few years ago, for instance, a few months after a friend whom I had met through a writers' group lost her battle with breast cancer – a battle that had never prevented her from reaching out to support me in either my writing or my own never ending struggles with my health – when I decided to drop a note to her widower, whom I had met just once, briefly.

Because I had often heard it said that one of the most excruciating times after the loss of a loved one is the period when the memorials have been held and the condolence cards have been sent and the rest of the world returns to tending its own business while you're left alone with your grief, I decided that letting him know that I was still missing my friend, too, would be a way of paying forward her many kindnesses to me. One last chance to thank her, I thought as I dropped the note in the mailbox, and then promptly forgot that I'd sent it. Until I received his note back. He was missing her too, he said. In fact, he would *always* be missing her, he said. And furthermore, he said, he wanted to make it perfectly clear that she was the *only* woman he would *ever* be interested in missing in the way that he missed her.

Okay then. I still cringe every time I recall the words in his note, and although I spent some time contemplating writing again with an "Ohmygod, you completely misunderstood!," I soon came to realize that the more I protested, the less he would believe me, and so I had no choice but to let it go. Or, at least, had no choice but to *try* to let it go, but what I've discovered in the time since is that that's not so easily done. Which is why, while – despite the periodic bouts of cringing – I still don't regret that I reached out in kindness that time, what I do regret is that his response to that kindness has kept me, on occasion, from reaching out again.

On *this* occasion, for instance: It's a year or so later and I'm sitting in my car at Lake Michigan's edge in the hour before sunrise, where I often start my day and where, on this particular day, Beethoven's ghost is playing "Moonlight Sonata" all over the beach. The world is swathed in black velvet, with little light in the sky, save for a crescent moon that's sending a circle of nacre down to float upon the water. Lightning is flashing every now and then – postcards mailed home from last night's storm, now that it's moved on – and after a time, the horizon exhales its first breath of light, until, suddenly, the entire span of the sky is cast in a delft shade of blue with patches of pearl drifting across it. The stage has been set for a clarinet or trumpet solo, smooth and seamless and shivering with grace, and I slip

Gershwin's "Summertime" into my CD player just so that I can keep playing and replaying its opening lament.

It had been summertime, I find myself thinking then, when I first met David and Ken. A summertime a few years after my law school graduation, not long after my illness had ambushed me once again, knocking the breath out of me to the point where I'd had to leave the career and the relationship and the life I'd been creating and move back to my parents' home. David had been a close friend of my brother-in-law's since college and, when my parents had learned that he and his partner, Ken, were in town for a visit, they'd invited them, along with my sister and brother-in-law, to dinner. A dinner which I attended bedecked head to toe in embarrassment and shame.

Since returning to my home town, I had rarely left the house, even during the short periods when I had enough energy to do so, so filled was I with dread at the prospect of running into someone I knew, or had once known, and finding myself coming up against the inevitable, "So, what are you *up* to these days?" Despite all that my head understood about the enormity of the health battle I was waging, and had been waging for most of my life, my heart continued to insist that "FAILURE" was stamped across my forehead. After all, was how my internal argument went, I had only one thing on my To Do list – "Recover!" – and I couldn't seem to get it checked off.

It seemed the worst kind of defeat to me to have made it all the way to my law school graduation through an obstacle course of two operations and three additional hospital stays only to now find myself back where I'd started. And that sense of defeat was only heightened by the fact that the illness I was battling was so poorly understood that those few friends I still had (those who hadn't already found all of this too difficult to relate to and quietly tiptoed away) had long ago given up on trying to understand it. Which is why *I* had long ago given up on trying to explain it. "I'mfinehowareyou?" I would say when cornered, always racing to deflect the focus of any conversation away from myself, so that it sometimes felt as if I were engaged in a perpetual game of hot potato.

But David and Ken, I rapidly discovered that night, weren't playing. "No, not yet," each of them said when I tried to toss the potato to him, and "Really, *tell* us," they said, and then they asked everything it appeared they genuinely wanted to know, about how it felt, this illness, and not only this illness, but the fear that was its Siamese twin, and about what it had done to my body, and not only to my body, but to my life as well. And then we talked about HIV and AIDS and how like that battle mine was, and by the time the meal was through and my mother was serving the sorbet, I had stopped being lost.

It was summertime, the evening of that dinner, but that's not why I find myself thinking of it as I sit on the beach on that years later morning, with a new day developing like a photograph in a dark room around me and Gershwin's composition shimmying and reshimmying its way to a moan. The reason I find myself thinking of that dinner at that moment is that I learned just last night that David has lost Ken

to his own lengthy health battle. And so, as soon as I return home from the beach, I sit down and write him an e-mail, telling him how much their kindness at that dinner had meant to me, and how much it had stayed with me since, and how much I wish I had told both of them that at the time, and how much he is in my thoughts now. I spend a long time composing that e-mail and then I revise it and reread it and reread it once more before guiding my cursor toward "Send." Which is when the thought of my friend's widower's response to that other note resurfaces in my mind and I find myself clicking on "Save to Drafts" instead.

There is no danger, of course, of David's misconstruing my intentions in the way that my friend's widower had, and yet that startling response to what I had thought was a simple gesture of kindness has made me so second guess myself that I find myself hesitating to send this e-mail anyway. I have seen David and Ken only once since that long ago dinner, this time at my niece's Bar Mitzvah party shortly before Ken died, where, in the middle of a room pulsing with gyrating teenagers and Klezmering musicians and to-and-fro-ing waiters and shouting-to-be-heard adults, we'd managed only a cursory chat. Will David think it's strange for me to still be remembering that dinner? I find myself wondering. Will he think it startling even? I don't know.

I can't be sure, because one thing I do know for sure is that my years of being so frequently side lined, of looking at the world so often from a distance, have left me seeing it differently from the way that most people do. Have left me changed to the point where it sometimes feels as if I've developed something akin to the bioluminescence which I recently read is used by the Western Grebe, a bird that lives alongside large, deep lakes in the western half of North America, to enable it to forage for food at night, locating even the most elusive of fish in total darkness. It appears that I've developed a type of bioluminescence for locating places where kindness is needed.

Maybe that was unavoidable, given how many times I've been in need of kindness myself, and, in any case, I'm at peace with having developed this somewhat odd faculty, but if that cringe-inducing response I'd received had taught me anything, it was that it's a faculty that I have to think twice before using if I don't want to leave a trail of raised eyebrows in my wake. And so I leave it there, in drafts, that e-mail to David, a frozen embryo of kindness that, as it turns out, I will never allow to develop to full term. I have regretted that decision every time I have thought of it since.

What I don't regret is having acquired that bioluminescence, because it enables me to zero in not only on the places where kindness might be needed, but on those where it's being committed as well, even when the person committing it is doing so hidden from view. Take a man I'll call Gus, for instance. A small, prickly man who is the manager of the grocery store at the center of my town, he's prone to long, gloomy silences and short, staccato bursts of speech that are designed to cement his reputation as a curmudgeon. "How was your vacation?" I once asked him after he'd been away for a couple of weeks, and "Terrible," he answered. Pause. "It ended." And: "How did you know to choose that horse?" I asked him after I'd heard that he'd betted on I'll Have Another when it won the Kentucky Derby, and "By its name, of course," he answered. "I'm a drunk." And so.

And so you might wonder how it is that I've made such a habit of asking him anything at all, and the answer to that is that he lets me shop early, before the store opens. "Open at 7:00 a.m.," says the sign on the door, but he's there hours before that, having driven from his home in the city to this suburb twenty or so miles north of it, and has developed a policy of allowing anyone who needs to to roam its empty aisles. I don't know how I discovered that policy, but it was a gift to me, since I'm up with the sun and since my unreliable energy and ever present pain make it a challenge for me to shop when the store's aisles are as crammed as they quickly become once its doors have officially opened.

And so there I am, once a week or so, pushing a cart through its preternatural calm, and there he is, interrupting the flow of his morning routine – of his transactions with delivery truck drivers and his review of the stock and his setting up of the cash registers and his arranging of displays – to ring up my groceries. And not only mine, but those of anyone who might be in need of that kindness. One morning, that included a wobbly man who arrived at the store on a wobbly bicycle and who then proceeded to narrate his journey through its aisles in a fulminant bellow. "Where are the Snyder's PRETZELS, Gus? I LIKE Snyder's pretzels." ("Aisle five, buddy. Just for you.") "Soup is GOOD FOOD and it's GOOD to BUY GOOD FOOD, right Gus? ("You bet, big guy. You go for it.") And so on. Until he had made his way back to the cash register, where Gus Rubik's cubed his selections into a single bag so that they would fit into the wobbly basket of that wobbly bicycle and, with a final "SEE YOU MAYBE TOMORROW AND MAYBE NOT," he teetered off into his day.

On another morning, a wild eyed woman staggered through the door wearing a shrieking infant, like an alarm clock with no "off" button, swaddled to her chest. "Formula," she croaked. "I've *got* to find a new *formula*." To which Gus responded by looking up from the invoice he was checking. And by shrugging. And cocking his head. And pointing. And saying: "Jack Daniels. Aisle three." And turning his attention back to his invoice, while I watched the woman realize that she still remembered how to laugh.

On yet another morning, I saw him carrying bags of groceries out to a man and a woman in a small dented white car and knew immediately who they were. Immigrants from Mexico, here working at landscaping and house cleaning jobs, their photograph had been on the front page of the local newspaper the week before when their five-year-old daughter had been killed by a car run amok on the main street of our town. I don't know how it came to be that Gus had gotten in touch with them, or that he had arranged for them to come to the store before it opened so that he could give them this food, but there he was, silently carrying it out to them, bag after bag, his face a "Do Not Even THINK About Commenting" sign.

Which didn't stop me from having a complimentary com-

ment plastered straight across my own face when he came back inside. "Yeah?" he said when he saw it, already hurrying over to straighten a display of paper goods that were on sale. "Well, you can give 'em a million bucks and they still don't get their baby back." And then this small man in a small store in the middle of a town in the middle of America, who will certainly leave this Earth without ever having had his name heralded in the headlines or ricocheted around the Twitterverse, or having been the star of a reality show, turned back to grumbling about how someone had put the paper towels where the toilet paper was supposed to go.

> # I think that sometimes kindness rides a Harley. That sometimes kindness dresses in black leather...

He's right, of course. They still don't get their baby back. But they do, at least, get something. Something that matters, I believe. A *Don't let go.* A *Here. Hang onto this.* A *You're not alone here after all.* Weak? I don't think so. *I* think that sometimes kindness rides a Harley. That sometimes kindness dresses in black leather, pulls on hip boots and a helmet and flexes the anaconda tattooed on the bulge of its bicep before gunning its motor, snorting smoke out its muffler, and screeching off to change the world.

In fact, I know that it does, because I saw it happen just the other day when I was stopped at a red light and looked up to see it, that Harley, complete with a helmeted and hip booted and tattooed man atop it, stopped at the red light facing me. And setting out into the crosswalk directly in front of it was a white haired sigh of a woman, slumped down in a wheelchair that was being pushed by a nurse. A white-haired sigh of a woman who, I could see even from my distance, was making a point of looking anywhere but at that man on that motorcycle. Who was, in fact, doing everything she could to disappear. Until she was directly in front of him, which is when he said something to her which I, of course, couldn't hear. It was something that mattered, though, that much I know, because, right there, as I watched, that woman grew a face. Grew a life story. Sat up straighter in her chair. So that, by the time she'd reached the opposite side of the street, she'd left a trail of years strewn across the asphalt behind her. Kindness.

Exactly what I'd found waiting for me on that afternoon just over a year ago when I'd limped out the front door of that hospital fifty or so miles from my home, tested and tortured and tossed back into the world, and when that valet parking attendant had driven my car up to the entrance and, stepping out of it and holding the door open for me, had said, "Everything gonna be jus' fine, you'll see. *Jus'* fine," and when I had driven away believing him.

Michael S. Moos

The Color of Passing Time

Pale morning sunlight touches the dry garden
moving deeper into the dreamless sleep you sometimes enter,
hiding in the interiors of your bones.
Sometimes you see tracks of small animals, arriving
not with hope, but with a species of remembered knowledge.
Limestone steps lead to the river's careful edge, where
the yellow willows endure, hanging like a brooding benediction
under the stillness of the sky, as the slow morning light
reaches toward the surface of your life, flowing
below the sheath of its unhealed scars. Like the river, silent
beneath the skin of its marbled gray ice, waiting
for a cleansing wind, shifting endlessly with the seasons,
the rising and falling drift of the continent. Or desire,
always waiting to return, the way a glimpse of happiness
comes into the body of its own accord, then slips into the wind
and disappears again.

Untitled

Jenny Bye
encaustic collage on board

Desert Poem (Shifting Sands)

Steve Joy
mixed media on panel

Nancy Lael Braun

We Didn't Have Air-Conditioning

The red-hot July and August
we played house in an apartment
downtown above the printshop
of the Galesburg Register-Mail,
a relentless chunka chunka
going on below. Worried about
our cats who were moping around,
pink tongues poked out,
I saddled them with wet washcloths,
myself in a swimsuit doused at intervals.

You were at work; I at loose ends
between jobs. I never even thought
how stupid it was to have the oven on,
trying to cook up bagels for a surprise.
Boiling water was roiling, steaming up
the kitchen while the dough over-rose —
and I lost it, fuckshit-goddamming
through the window screens.
Bread dough went up from my hands
and stuck to the ceiling. The cats cowered.

Why did the heat break that evening,
cool snaking in, pulling us out the kitchen
window onto the black tar rooftops,
cushiony and still radiant but allowing
our flip-flopped feet to walk, then run,
among the chimneys and silver vents,
the newsprinter drumming away beneath.
The naked cats flicked their tails
as I told my story, the breeze a faint rebuke.
I swore the apartment was contaminated
now; you said prayers can be odd-shaped.

Machine Painting 6

Mark Kochen
acrylic on canvas

Luiza Flynn-Goodlett

American Dialectic

In Concord, in Westchester, in Belle Meade,
pool covers are lifted, sodden leaves netted
and flung onto the grass. Sprinklers shoot

up, a coronation crowd, and cascade droplets,
like handfuls of petals, into suburban air. Trees
unhunch, sprout tender greens. Infants shuck

the husks of mothers' thighs, emerge suckling.
Dictionaries molder, exhale linguistic musk
as children bisect the garden, sparklers spitting

blue flame, exclamations truncated, unadorned.
We sharpen pencils, mar sheets in their service,
preserve verbs, the semicolon's grace, velvety

adjectives, the snug chamber of a clause. Once
outcasts ourselves – egg-shaped and awkward –
we know the savagery of wire-rims and braces,

the queer buds of breasts. So we hold
syllables, savor each, then stack words –
Lincoln Logs – into what looks like home.

Norma Wilson

The White Wing

The Keeper of the White Wing
rode ill with pneumonia
to save his people.
Bearing a white flag
he sought peace.
But others would fight.

At Wounded Knee
the soldiers' guns
killed for hours.
That December day
two hundred fifty Lakotas
and twenty-five soldiers died.

After the slaughter
a blizzard flew
from the North.

As an elder shouted,
"The wing, the wing!"
the gravedigger threw
the blood-stained white wing
into the burial trench.

A century later,
white-winged birds
ride the North winds
soaring over the curving river
glistening with sunlight,
the checkered fields
of green and brown,
the river banks
with umbrella-like shade
that once
belonged to all.

Even birds sharing seeds
seem to know
that Earth's abundance
is the white wing of peace,
falling to earth
as flakes of snow.

Big Sioux River, Union County

Nancy Losacker
mosaic

Summertime

Larry Roots
acrylic on canvas

Mercedes Lawry

Flannery's Peacocks

What glum love excuses the greed of forgetfulness?
In the ancient, layered light of dusk,
across boiled wool clouds, crows natter in their vast passage.

Time fell out of my hands, not cupped enough,
not tight in fists, unable to save or rescue.

The motion of my grief is a swell.
The duration of my grief is infinite and unknown.

I wear my solitude as strata, peel and unpeel,
clammy or chilled, always as if a wind
might blow through, a tremor might buckle my knees.

It is my own voice that is so harsh,
like the scrape of a siren breaking dream,
like ailing cats or Flannery's peacocks,
like anyone left behind.

Acqua Alta

Kate Bullard Adams

It wasn't the first time they'd been to Venice. They'd visited four, maybe five times before – neither one of them could remember – and twice they'd stayed for a month. But it was the first time she'd seen a tourist in San Marco taking a picture of the ground rather than the basilica or the *campanile* or, her favorite, the clock tower, whose blue-enameled face, studded with stars and the signs of the zodiac, softened the sting of time.

She followed the angle of the camera and saw that it was aimed, on this clear, sunny day, at a shallow puddle of water near the basilica. High water. *Acqua alta.* But wasn't that just in the winter? And this was June, almost July, as evidenced by the swarms of tourists and her sweat-damp blouse.

She pointed the water out to her "counterpart." At late middle age, calling each other boyfriend and girlfriend was ridiculous, and a tongue-tied hotel clerk had come up with counterpart, which seemed suitably mature, and suitably vague. And it made them laugh.

With the dazed look that had become the norm, he nodded, then followed her toward the sculpture of the tetrarchs mounted on a corner of the basilica. They no longer felt the need to go inside the church – or the Doge's Palace or the Frari or the Accademia. Instead, they sought out the particular places and details, like this porphyry rendering of the four Roman emperors that were special favorites, old friends.

On this day, tourists surrounded the tetrarchs, leaning against the walls on which they were mounted or sitting on the steps at their feet. Only when she raised her camera did the sightseers seem to realize they were near something special. They turned to look at the beautiful purplish red carving, the two pairs of rulers, whose stony faces and rigid postures offered no reaction.

"Let's get you in here," she said, guiding him toward the tetrarchs. Obligingly, the tourists moved aside. "Smile," she said, but his mouth hardly moved, and she tried not to think

how much his stiff bearing and fixed countenance resembled the sculpture. "Got it," she said, as she clicked the camera and froze them in time. "Back to the hotel?" At his nod, she turned to carve a path through the people and pigeons, skirting the occasional pool of water that rose through narrow weep holes, slowing her pace to match his. From atop the clock tower, the two bronze Moors – one old, the other, young – bent from hinged waists to strike the hour. His shoes scuffed like sandpaper across the worn stone of the square.

When she'd first met him, he'd been something of a tetrarch himself. He was managing partner of one of Atlanta's biggest law firms, and on her first visits there, she'd been dazzled by the trappings of his position: his office and his car, the people he knew and the parties they attended. Even more dazzling was his library, filled with favorite novels that he'd arranged alphabetically by author and that he pulled from the shelves with the same sureness of purpose that had made her say yes when, during his third visit to Savannah, he asked if she'd like to come to his hotel room after dinner. She didn't leave until he checked out.

That wasn't her usual style. In her other relationships, including her marriage, intellectual compatibility had come first, then a gradual warming up to the physical part of things. And her first reaction to him physically had been one of dismay. "What have you done to me?" was her unspoken cry to the friend who'd set them up. She opened her door on that long-ago Saturday afternoon and greeted the heavyset man with the sleepy eyes and the thinning hair and the eyebrows whose hairs went every which way. He was dressed in slacks, a striped shirt, and a sweater vest that gave a graceful droop to his paunch. He looked very corporate and very conventional. And he looked very old.

But then he held out an orchid, its spike laden with waxy white blooms. And then he introduced himself to her teenaged children without saying anything that embarrassed anybody. He made comfortable conversation throughout a long walk and during dinner at the restaurant where he had taken care of the reservation. Afterwards, when she played the new CD she'd bought just for that evening, they slow danced in the living room. And by the time he left, after he'd kissed her on the cheek and given her one more chance to breathe in his warm, gingery scent, she'd forgotten that he was nine years older than she was and realized with some surprise, and a little alarm, that she was sorry to see him go.

The hotel was only a few bridges and a couple of *campos* from San Marco. In the old days, he'd have kept up with her, carried along by the current of people flowing through the *calle*, excited anew by this most improbable of places. How had this city, a mirage-like marvel of stone, wood, and brick, built its way out of the water? And would the water eventually win it back? During their previous visits, this impermanence, the sense of living on borrowed time, had caused them to pick up their pace. But his knees were bothering him, and she had to remind herself to slow down, and every so often they had to stop, breaking up the flow of people like a snag in a river. Their snag was a minor one, though, and passersby seemed hardly to notice. There was nothing special, she was starting to learn, about older people getting left behind.

Their hotel had just reopened after an eighteen-month renovation, most of which had been cosmetic. The concierge, however, had made special mention of the huge holding tank beneath the ground floor that was upgraded to handle the water that had begun to encroach on the lobby. "The Grand Canal, we love," he had explained, "when it is outside."

They loved the Grand Canal, too, and went out to enjoy it at the waterside bar. The boats! So many! Gondolas, their *ferros* glinting in the sun. *Vaporettos* zigzagging from one stop to the next. Delivery boats with cargo piled to precarious heights. Water taxis showing off their speed. The *carabinieri,* the trash boats, the *ambulanza*, the *guardia di finanza* – they'd even seen some kayaks near the Cipriani. And, miracle of miracles, they'd never seen any of them run into each other.

He used to have a boat that he kept down in Florida. At one time, fishing had been his passion, and he told stories of going out into the gulf for swordfish or tuna, or simply dropping a line off the side of a bridge. They'd walked around several of the marinas in Savannah, and he'd picked up information about their policies and pricing. Politely noncommittal, she had smiled and said nothing. Maybe for that reason, the boat continued to sit in Florida. And finally, after years of renting slips and replacing dead batteries, he had sold it.

Despite his estrangement from the water he'd once loved, the intricate bustle of the canal brightened his mood, and with the help of her Bellini and his Lillet, they engaged in something close to a conversation. She asked him questions. He reminisced about his fishing expeditions out of Mexico, his Hemingway-esque adventures in the gulf. His hands, still big and supple, pulled marlin from the stream of memory. His

narrowed eyes commanded some distant view. And through the soft scrim of gin, she could see the man she'd fallen in love with, a lion lazing in the sun after a successful day's hunt.

They'd gotten the diagnosis about six months ago, two years after he'd retired and moved to Savannah. It didn't come as a surprise. They'd known that something was wrong: the arm that began holding itself at a right angle; the big, bold handwriting that started to disappear; the brain that couldn't deal with a bank statement. But when he began falling out of bed, sudden crashes in the night that yanked her eyes open and hammered her heart, she did some research. There was something called REM sleep behavior disorder. Sometimes it was a condition in and of itself. But usually, it was a symptom of something else. And usually that was Parkinson's.

They felt like they were handling it well. They went together to his appointments with the neurologist, and, despite the trembling limbs and frozen faces that surrounded them, they'd stayed all day at the Parkinson's symposium. On the weekends they went to movies and got together with friends. They still lingered in bed on Saturday mornings, drinking coffee and looking out at the lemon trees before they made love. But during the week, in the evenings, when they sat down to dinner and it was just the two of them, it was hard to ignore how very little they had to say.

> How had this city, a mirage-like marvel of stone, wood, and brick, built its way out of the water? And would the water eventually win it back?

In the early years, there'd been lots to talk about. She taught English at the college; he loved to read. He told her about the rare manuscripts he used to collect, the auctions he'd frequented in New York. She tried out new course material on him.

Now, he didn't have the concentration to finish anything longer than a magazine article, and she didn't watch television, which took up more and more of his time. It didn't take long to exhaust any scraps of news about the neighbors or their children, none of whom lived nearby. The cat provided only limited material.

She fell back on music, and as long as she remembered to put on a CD before dinner, they had Bach or Debussy or Dianne Reeves to cover up the quiet. But if she forgot, the two of them were on their own. She'd secretly hope the dog next door would start barking. Or maybe the neighbor's son would turn up his electric guitar. Otherwise, it was just the silverware clinking and the ceiling fan's tick. And the maddening burst of sound when he chewed, the ragged, obligatory stutter of an old sewing machine.

While *La Mesopanditissa's* gaze was directed away from her grown son's suffering, the man-child could glimpse it from the corner of his eye. He could see what was coming. It was only a matter of time.

While he rested at the hotel, she took the *vaporetto* to the Salute, the big Baroque wedding cake of a church that anchored one end of the Grand Canal. As close as it was to San Marco — just a few minutes away on the other side of the canal — the Salute was rarely crowded, and its spacious, dimly lit interior felt like a cool hand on her forehead.

The church had been built in the 1600s as a tribute to the Virgin Mary for saving Venice from the plague. In honor of her intervention, it housed a painting called *La Madonna della Salute*, the Madonna of Health. But this madonna was not one of the fulsome, fair-skinned Marys who inhabited most of the other Venetian churches. She was a Byzantine icon brought from Crete with a long, steep nose, umber eyes, and even darker skin. Also known as *La Mesopanditissa*, she wore a simple red gown and turban, and the child, really a miniature man, who sat upright in the crook of her arm, had the same dusky skin and solemn gaze. They were eloquent in their austerity.

On her previous pilgrimages, which had been in January, she had found the icon sequestered in a small room off the sanctuary. But today, illuminated by their gold halos and gilt frames, the mother and child were clearly visible, enthroned on the high altar in an open chapel on the other side of the church. She followed the ambulatory that curved around the petaled swirls of mosaic floor beneath the dome until she came to the altar, where an organist and a violinist were playing. She joined the small audience and studied the madonna in this different, grand setting.

It was as if *La Mesopanditissa* had moved to Hollywood. Sculpted at the time of the church's construction, the altar surrounding the mother and the child was a scene of high drama. Above their heads, an oversized Mary, draped in voluptuous folds of fabric, held a plump baby Jesus on her hip. With the help of a weapon-wielding cherub, cheered on by the patron saints, she drove out the cowering female figure of the plague. *La Mesopanditissa* and her son appeared politely unimpressed by these histrionics. Amid the altar's frenzied swirl of stone, they seemed alone in a way they hadn't when she'd seen them before in the small quiet chamber.

If a kinship were to be found, it was with the wooden crucifix to their right. It was similar in its reserve, its frugality of expression. The finished body of Christ needed no embellishment. While *La Mesopanditissa's* gaze was directed away from her grown son's suffering, the man-child could glimpse it from the corner of his eye. He could see what was coming. It was only a matter of time.

With a final flourish of the violinist's bow, the concert ended. There was a smattering of applause. She got up to leave. On her way out, as was her custom, she stopped at the votives. She dropped a euro in the box, picked up one of the small red candles. It was difficult to light, its too-short wick hard to hold close enough to the neighboring flame. Finally, it caught. She took a long last look at the distant madonna. Salute. Health. A city saved. But not her own son.

She left the church, walked down the broad cascade of steps. At the bottom, a beggar crouched, the pavement damp beneath his feet. She reached in her pocket for another euro. "*Grazie, signora*," said a thin, wavering voice. "*Prego*," she whispered in reply. She turned in the direction of the approaching *vaporetto*. There was no way of avoiding the vast pool of water in between.

Mont St. Michel, Normandy, France

Jack Bristow
photograph

La Bendición De Ser Abnormal

Angelica A. Mercado
oil on canvas

Alyssa Mazzarella

Birth

Everything was lit white:
the gowns, the skin beneath

the hair shaved without explanation,
the cotton caps, the bed

they strapped my arms to
when they screamed *push*,

the pillow held to my face.
This doesn't concern you, they said.

You will have children
of your own someday, they said.

Then, undrunk milk throbbed
in my silted breasts.

A hand aimed a heat lamp at stitches
between my bent, open legs

and a janitor walked in
without knocking.

Willie VerSteeg

Love Poem

If I loved you
in terms of a metaphor
of the body unspooling,
it would be my arms,
how they oozed out
of my hollow sleeves
into coils on the floor.
Isn't that
what we come to love
about early love:
impractical spectacle,
unflinching gesture,
the cat leaving a dead bird
in your spot on the bed?
I've woken
before you,
and the morning
is both warm and blue.
It is always
at this time, when I want to say,
It will never be the same –
no. Closer:
It will always be different.
And some morning delirium –
My arms will grow back.
That part
will not make sense to you.
For that, and other reasons,
I stay quiet, though
there was a time
I would've woken you.

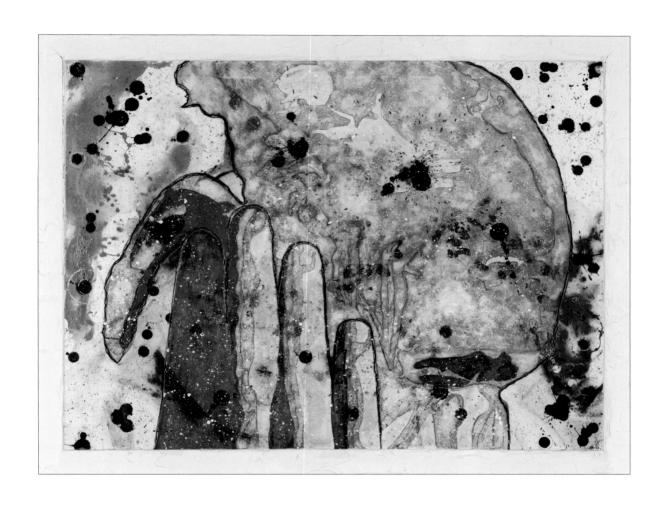

Plaques and Tangles

Brian Joel Damon
acrylic and tempera on canvas

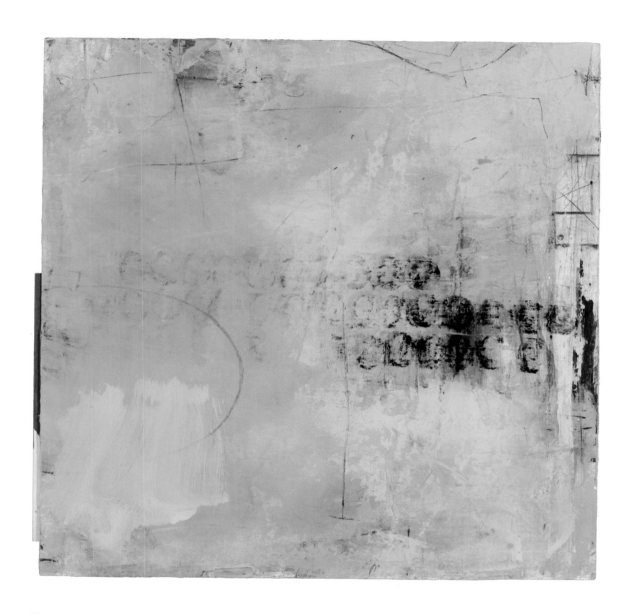

#33

Rick Johns
acrylic, graphite, charcoal & stir stick on wood panel

Lisa Beans

Second Snow

Last night, a light snow mixed
with corn dust in a combine's light.

Tonight, I can't see the road.
(Will you know when I leave?)

Snow in my headlights,
the illusion of moving backward.

A van resting on its side,
flashing its underbelly:

the difference between
alone and lonely becomes clear.

Once a coyote, standing under a light,
watched me for a moment too long.

Do you know how I've prayed for you?
Fervently. (This time, come to me.)

How quickly the Platte River froze,
how quickly the stillness and fear came.

Coming Home

David Evans

"Be kind to yourself, dear – to our innocent follies. Forget any sounds or touch you know that did not help you dance. You will come to see that all evolves us."

– Rumi

In his well-known anthology, *Crazy Wisdom*, the Buddhist meditation teacher, Wes Nisker, says: "Climb into the balcony of your consciousness, and find a seat. Once you see yourself from up there, everything takes a different look."

What Wisker is saying - drawing mostly from an Eastern tradition that reaches back more than 2,500 years – has been expressed by many others. The psychologist Carl Jung identified four stages of life, the last one being the Stage of the Spirit, in which we're capable of stepping back from our mind and seeing things the way they truly are. Oscar Wilde said, "To become a spectator of one's own life is to escape the suffering of life."

"Lower" Fourth Street. The Virginia Hotel and neighboring Thelander Drugs were both functioning, in part, as "houses of ill fame." Photo taken in 1940.

Courtesy of the Sioux City Public Museum

Moving back to the Sioux City area, after living elsewhere for 50 years, has prompted me to have a look at how the landscape where I spent my youth has changed, and also how I got from who I was then to who I am now. At 75 – my new perspective of awareness – I'm discovering that things do take, as Wisker says, "a different look."

As I move around the city, observing, and talking with school friends and others, I'm becoming more and more aware of two main threads running through my life. One thread might be described by using such words as *competitive, reckless,* and *obsessive;* and the other one, by such words as *contemplative, self-conscious,* and *creative.* Those two threads, as I'm seeing them now, are more tightly interwoven – not only with each other but with the physical settings in which they originated – than I ever thought.

. . . I sometimes drive to the two main neighborhoods I lived in: the first – and by far the more formative of the two – from age 7 to 15; and the second, through high schoool graduation.

Courtesy of the Sioux City Public Museum

Woodrow Wilson Junior High School.
Photo taken in the late 1920s or early 1930s.

A good starting point is at Fourth and Floyd Boulevard. *Floyd Boulevard?* The phrase has a jarring sound for me, since in my time it was called *Wall Street*. Fourth Street (where my older brother Jerry and I delivered papers in the early 50s), these days looks surprisingly tidy and appealing, compared to the "red-light district" (or *Lower Fourth*) it used to be known as.

    . . . I drive north, and a few blocks later I come to the south edge of my first main neighborhood, a place where my junior high school, Woodrow Wilson – with its conspicuously tall smoke stack – used to sit. Irving Elementary School now occupies the same space. *Irving?* That was the grade school I went to when it was not far from Central High School. Driving by this new Irving, I picture in my mind Woodrow's playground and its high fence, and especially the street between the playground and the school. I ran my first official races on that street.

    Those three Woodrow years were crucial to my identity as a person. All kids need to establish some degree of status among their peers. I got mine almost exclusively from my athletic abilities. I was a fairly shy kid, except for when I was doing something athletic. I was quick to please others and quick to feel the sting of any criticism, inept at practical tasks, and mediocre as a student. One day my teacher mentioned, in front of all of my classmates, that I had a "math block." For a long time I assumed that she was tired of me dragging down my classmates. (How easy it's been all my life for my mind to lean toward the negative!) But anymore, I see that she was probably just stating a fact.

    . . . Continuing north on Floyd Boulevard/Wall Street a few blocks more – downhill and then uphill – I come to the heart of that first main neighborhood, and the old brick house my family lived in, on the railroad bluff.

    I was the middle kid in my family, with a younger brother and sister and an older brother and sister. My older brother (by five years) was a good athlete and student and also

outgoing, ambitious, and as we used to say, *level-headed*. My mother was quiet and serious. Given my tendency to take risks as well as my impracticality, I can understand now why we were sometimes at odds.

    I both revered and feared my dad. He was a big imposing man who had been an excellent golfer and bowler. (I was born when he was 30, so I wasn't able to watch him playing games in his prime – a fact that I regret). Having quit school after the eighth grade, he was a self-educated intellectual in love with books. A driven man – I remember him saying more than once that "a person should find something to be good at" – he spent much of his time, after work and on weekends, not so much with my siblings and me, but reading, or writing at his small basement desk. For 30 years he would work as a pressman in the *Sioux City Journal* building (now a parking lot), and then get hired by his international pressmen's union, as the Managing Editor of their magazine. He, my mother, and younger brother and sister (my older sister and brother had left home, and I was starting college in Sioux Falls) were living in Pressman's Home, Tennessee when, just as his writings were becoming known in the world of labor education, he died suddenly of a heart attack. He was 52.

    The only brick house on Wall Street, as our family proudly called it, is still there on the hill street, minus the white picket fence and the creaking, wooden-slatted porch swing. The

Courtesy of the Sioux City Public Museum as part of the archives of the Sioux City Journal.

Press from the Sioux City Journal similar to the one that Art Evans worked on as a pressman for the Journal. Photo taken by George Newman sometime between 1945 and 1954.

few things inside the house that I remember, I remember well: the book shelves full of hundreds of my dad's books; his grey, vinyl recliner; the unfinished basement; the washing machine and the time when, messing around with a friend, I got my right wrist caught in its ringer – the wild panic, the dark scar on my wrist that lasted for years; my dad's wooden desk and swivel desk chair, his old black typewriter; and the shower, where, Caruso-style, he sang arias from operas, or recited soliloquies from *Hamlet*.

Just north of the house I'm glad to see the vacant lot is still there, even though it's too weedy to be used for pole vaulting. My brother taught me to vault, and we built our vaulting pit at the west end of the lot: a wooden box sunk into the ground, for planting the pole (a bamboo one with the black plumbers' tape wrapped on the top end for a grip), a landing pit full of dirt we'd keep digging up with a spade (for a relatively soft landing), the uprights made of two-by-fours, with long nails pounded in them at six-inch intervals, all the way to 10 feet, or 10-6.

Pole vaulting became an obsession. I remember the notebook I had, in which I meticulously kept track of my progress, and dates: 7 feet, 7-6, 8-0, 8-6, 9. . . . I'm thinking now that my habit of keeping track of things as a writer (such as images in poems), may have begun with those notebook entries.

My love of teaching may also have begun in that vacant lot. I gladly taught my friend Jerry Nyreen to vault, and then, astonished and jealous, had to watch him out-vault me consistently, even though he didn't practice nearly as much as I did, and lacked my speed and technique, but had more arm-strength for the pull-up.

Most of my memories of those Woodrow/Wall Street bluff years are positive, and most have to do with sports and competition – football, baseball, swimming, and ice skating. Running was an early obsession. I can easily see myself sprinting at full speed, alone or in races, through cindered alleys and on sidewalks, uphill and downhill and level, often glancing down at my

knees as they pumped faster and faster. Fast enough, in fact, for me to have been the lead-off runner of the 1955 Central High Freshman relay team that broke two six-year-old records in the Sioux City Relays.

I could never get enough of the joy of flat-out sprinting. Robert Frost (who loved sports and games in his youth) said that "poetry is as good as it is dramatic." It's not surprising that throughout my career I've written quite a lot of poetry and prose about athletes in motion.

Yin and yang – those junior high years had plenty of it. It was in the early fall of my seventh grade year, when I began to feel what I thought was a pain in my chest when I took a deep breath. Already a worrier, I complained about my pain to my parents, who were puzzled. Finally my grandmother took me to a Dr. Dobson on the West Side, who concluded that I had Rheumatic Fever. He sent me home with a note to the Woodrow principal, saying that for "the balance of the semester" I was to avoid all strenuous activities, and to rest. At first I was in denial. One day after school the coach caught me playing in a pick-up basketball game, pulled me out and said: "Evans, if you don't do what the doctor says, you won't make it to 30." The words would haunt me for years, having come from a man I respected, and who also would tell me a couple of years later that I had the ability to be a 13-foot pole vaulter in high school – an exceptional height in the 50s.

I decided to obey the doctor's orders and stay inside in a classroom while my friends were in gym class, practicing basketball. But I found something to pass the time, and even got to liking it: drawing. Just sitting there alone, in a quiet classroom, drawing what I called "designs" on tablet paper, with a pencil or pen. The older I get the more aware I am of paradox. Dr. Dobson's diagnosis had been so

Central High School. Photo taken in 1957.

Courtesy of the Sioux City Public Museum

discouraging to a kid who loved sports, and yet, in retrospect, it was a very lucky thing for me. Those so-called "designs" I created, sitting alone in a quiet classroom, were probably a precursor of the hundreds of poems and other writings I've produced since my mid-20s – sitting alone, calmly, in other quiet rooms.

But drawing wasn't the only non-sports interest that was starting in my life.

I was becoming interested in poetry and literature, not only by hearing my dad quoting out loud from books and in the shower, but also by listening to his record of John Barrymore reciting cuttings from Shakespeare. Not only that, but I was beginning to realize that, like my dad, I had a good memory of words.

One day, at the age of 14 or 15, standing near the bookcase in the hallway by the front door. I pulled out a thick book from a shelf. Randomly turning pages, I stopped at a short poem called "Limited." The speaker of the poem (it was by Carl Sandburg, whom I'd never heard of) sounded like people I knew, and said that the train and everything on it would eventually become "scrap and rust," and "ashes," – even, by implication, "the man in the smoker" who, when he's asked, "where he is going . . . answers: 'Omaha.'" Seeing that word at the very end of the poem was like being struck with a baseball bat, it was so familiar, so local. Omaha was not far down the road! And passenger trains? Standing on the bluff, I'd seen a lot of them going by. The poem amazed me. I may even have sensed the irony: that the man in the smoker is not aware that he too will be reduced to ashes, even though he thinks he's just going to Omaha. But it didn't matter if I didn't understand exactly what Sandburg was up to. I started to "get" poetry long before I could paraphrase it.

Joseph Campbell spoke of peak moments in life. That moment in the hallway was one of mine.

I shared my new and quickly evolving interest in poetry with no one, not even my dad. (All these years later, however, I think that he probably sensed my inclination.) In the Sioux City macho working-class culture of the 1950s that I grew up in, poetry was for "egg heads" or "sissies." Sensing this, I began to sneak off alone to the public library, usually on Saturday mornings on the way to the YMCA (which was then close to the court house). I'd go downstairs to the listening room and put records of poets or actors reading poetry on the record player, and sit on the couch (as inconspicuously as possible), and listen. I couldn't get enough of Matthew Arnold's "Dover Beach," which I'd play over and over. It was the first poem that stuck in my memory; I can still recite it.

Soon I began to check out poetry records. Coming out of the library one day with a record tucked under my arm, I happened to walk by a big Central High football player, who asked me what I was carrying. I held up the record and he said to me: "What's that shit, poetry?" and walked away, snickering. There I was, holding something in my hand that was, for me, a treasure, and I'd just been told that it was shit.

Courtesy of David Evans

David's father, Art Evans, center, his wife, Jan, on his right, and her friend, Carolyn, on his left. Photo taken in 1955.

Such a comment would affect any kid, and especially a very sensitive one like me. Maybe I could call that moment near the library an *anti-peak moment* in my life.

. . . I keep driving north on the bluff, picturing the streetcar tracks (no trace remains) running along the east side and below the bluff. Wall Street used to stop abruptly at my friend Allen Cooley's house at the top of the street (the house is gone and Allen is dead), but these days the street keeps on going right over the bluff and down – a clever city engineering feat. Continuing on, I picture on my right the huge roundhouse, and the hissing steam engines. (All these, including the streetcars, have become since I left, and as Sandburg predicted in his poem, scrap and rust.) I used to show off around my friends by hopping a brief and perilous ride on a moving box car. I'm glad to see some trains are still there, and the sounds of them, if not the passenger trains (like the one that held the man in the smoker, who was heading for Omaha).

Also on my right, across the tracks, was the Sioux City Soos ball park, where my friends and I spent many nights in the late 40s and early 50s. It's gone too, and the little pond close by, where we swam in the summer and skated in the winter.

. . . Finally I come to Leeds, the second main neighborhood of my youth.

I turn left on Jefferson Street, where Leeds High used to be (a sprawling grade school now occupies the area). I drive around back and discover that the place where we practiced baseball is still there, as well as the football field, where we played our home games.

I get out of my car and look through the tall fence (like the one my dad used to watch me through, during football practice). It's all still alive in my memory: the 17-year-old senior left halfback, running ("in the shape of my father's hope" I would say in a poem 15 years later) for three touchdowns in the Homecoming game, beating Orange City, 20-6; my girlfriend Jan, one of the cheerleaders, leaping and singing the Leeds Lancer song; my dad, with other dads on the sideline, dutifully following the first-down chain; and my mother, up in the bleachers with the other mothers, yelling for their team, their boys.

> I left Sioux City over fifty years ago, but did I really leave? . . . In so many ways I'm still that kid on the railroad bluff, who couldn't get enough of running and pole vaulting . . .

. . . I leave the parking lot and drive back to Floyd Boulevard, then five or six blocks later, I turn left on Filmore Street and go north, and a couple of blocks later I come to the tiny house my family lived in for the three years before the move to Tennessee. Driving by the house, I too vividly picture our moving day, in the summer of 1955, when I was 15, and I feel a trace of the seething anger that I felt then, standing there in the driveway with my mother, unloading our Wall Street things into the garage. My anger came from having been, as I saw it, torn away from my Woodrow friends, who in a couple months would be attending Central High, The Castle on the Hill. Besides, track and field was being phased out at Leeds (but not before I got a blue ribbon in the Sioux City Sophomore Track Meet, pole vaulting for Leeds).

I still wonder why we left the brick house and moved to Leeds – to a strange neighborhood and into a tiny house much farther away from my dad's work at the *Journal*. I think now that, among other reasons, my dad had me in mind: he was very supportive of and attentive to my sports career, and he knew I'd have a better chance to stand out as an athlete in a smaller school. Not only that, but maybe I could get a college scholarship (he didn't have enough money to put me through). I was not nearly as independent and resourceful as my older brother, who had recently enlisted in the Air Force, and so a formal education for me would be a better route to a decent job.

By the time I glance over at the alley just west of our garage, the hint of any left-over anger has disappeared. Not more than a few days after our move to Leeds, I met Rich, living a few houses to the south. He would become a close

friend, and still is. And then within a week or so I met Jan, living a few houses to the north. Three years later we would get married. We recently had our 57th anniversary.

Life can happen fast for a kid after he turns 15. Those three years in Leeds are almost a blur in my memory. Going steady with Jan (the phrase is apparently defunct) consumed a lot of my time. My school work improved, and in my last year I made the honor roll. Sports continued, and now my focus was baseball and football. My dad's hope (if in fact a scholarship was what he had in mind for me) turned out well. I was recruited by several Division II schools and got a football scholarship and a good free start at college.

Another paradox: the move to Leeds made me assume (as stressed-out teenagers are known to assume) that all of my life was behind me and therefore I had no future. And yet, like Dr. Dobson's note to the principal at Woodrow, the move turned out to be a lucky thing for me.

One could do a lot worse than to take Rumi's advice: "Live life as if everything is rigged in your favor."

Thomas Wolfe said, "You can't go home again." I left Sioux City over fifty years ago, but did I really leave? Yes and no – another paradox. In so many ways I'm still that kid on the railroad bluff, who couldn't get enough of running and pole vaulting, and who had a problem with losing (these days, in pickleball); that kid who was quick to please others, and was inclined, like the small bird in the Frost poem, to "take / everything said as personal to himself"; that kid who worried about his heart; that kid who discovered drawing, and, thanks to his dad, began to fill his head with poetry.

Those two main threads in my life that I've been more keenly aware of since I came back – I see that they can't be separated from each other, anymore than yin can be separated from yang, joy from sorrow, fear from courage, hatred from love, or loss from gain. It all goes together and is one thing, a wholeness. I look around me, I read books, talk with family and friends, watch the nightly news, sports games, and other programs, and I realize that to be human is to be imperfect, and to suffer.

I've found that it helps to cultivate a sense of humor, and, for sure, to keep watching my mind. Buddhists make sense to me when they say that acceptance of yourself and of others, and of the moment, is the key to a modicum of contentment, even though acceptance is not easy to pull off. The philosopher Montaigne wrote centuries ago: "Our being is cemented with sickly qualities. Whoever should remove the seeds of these qualities from man would destroy the fundamental conditions of life." The Buddhist teacher, Pema Chodron, said something similar: "Our brilliance, our juiciness, our spiciness, is all mixed up with our craziness and our confusion, and therefore it doesn't do any good to try to get rid of our so-called negative aspects, because in that process we also get rid of our basic wonderfulness."

Back home again among these beautiful Loess Hills, after so many years of being away and not being away, I try to keep reminding my imperfect self: "Relax, Dave."

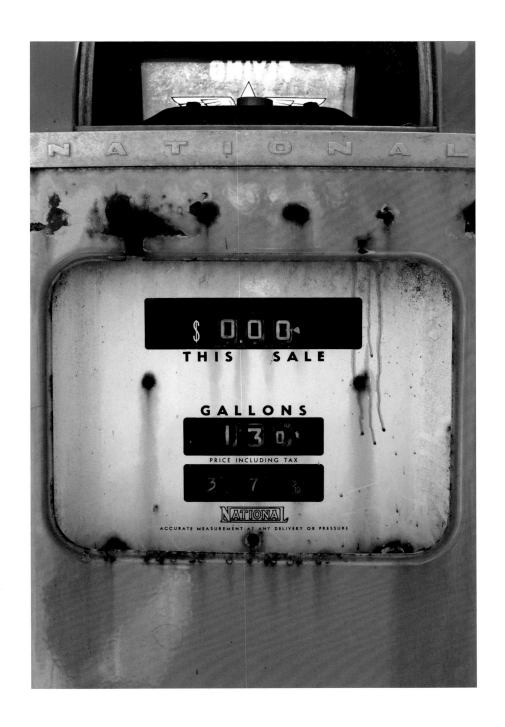

This Sale, Tamales Bay, CA, 2014

Ron Johns
photograph

David L. White

Conviction

Alles, was wir sehen, könnte auch anders sein.
Alles, was wir überhaupt beschreiben können, könnte
auch anders sein.

— Ludwig Wittegenstein

All morning I watch birds flee for their lives,
rushing before my mad-monkey of a dog.
The orange tree is still dotted with its
oranges but high where I cannot reach –
shriveled, rotting globes of gnats and weevils.

A great fire somewhere burns, leaves a haze
in the air, while reports in the paper
speak again of buried Babylon and
war, the retro-virus of history.

My dog swears on nothing she spins in the
grass, in the sun and flies with Quixote
wholeness at the summer burned artichoke plant.

Manifold shards of ten o'clock sun soaks
the roofs of houses, the palm of the sky
spreads blue over petals of lantana,
arching in reception, green leaves rise up
to know the day's full daylight.

How their need spurs them: they feed themselves with light,
but without eyes, do not know it as light;
undriven to name it or call upon
it as God or tell themselves that food
and God are different or same.

The orange tree, harboring its rotten universe
the lantana, fallen but uplifted,
the artichoke, consumed:
the light is not their food, but they feed from it
through endless translation.

Angelica A. Mercado

Tongues

My pa lost his tongue
somewhere between *el Río Grande*
y el desierto de Sonora
while chasing the American Dream
he did not notice its absence
until he opened his mouth
and what came out
was more white noise than melody
the tongue – now shrunken and dried,
sits in the sand like a raisin.
the day he gave his naturalizing oath
he was told to offer his heart as sacrifice
the temple – the country that replaced his tongue

he now speaks with a bleached organ,
stressing syllables foreign to him,
foreign like him
I tell him
Pa
you lost your tongue
but there is nothing
in this world that can
be replaced
only imitated
habla el español
que tú sabes
conduct melodies
in your own chest,
revive the heart,
the drum of life
it is still yours.

Me, I am different,
my supple tongue
speaks for two
los dioses aztecas
blessed me with a forked tongue,
like a double-headed serpent
it rises
each defending
her
territory,
her language,
her *voz.*

Shards 4

John Beckelman
fired ceramics, concrete, and mixed media

Michael Anania

Conjectures for an October Evening

Upriver, at Blair, bridgework
    shadowed across dull water,
        semis double-clutching the grade,
the wind, leaves clamoring
    down bluff channels, water-runs
        and stiff branches – if I could hold
it all in my hand, just so,
    not something gathered
        but caught hold of in passing
like twigs from choke –
    cherry thickets or foxtails
        along a fenceline, wild chamomile,
wood sorrel, its bitter touch,
    the wet taint of torn stems, river
        marl, their tastes deepening, word
after word. Somehow these
    things are tangible, not merely
        remembered but inventions
out of memory. Out my
    window now, pine needles stir,
        and there is no connection worth
noting between this agitation
    in the dark Illinois night
        and that proposed Nebraska,
except for the season, its
    edges, things reached out
        for and persistent change.

Tightrope

William Cass

Twice in the previous week, Doris had made it as far as the front door of the rectory before turning around. That morning, she managed to raise one hand to the knocker before hesitating and lowering her eyes to the small paper bag she held with the other. It was still, just past dawn. A small light blinked on in the back of the rectory and she held her breath. She could hear the sound of slippers shuffling inside on linoleum. She set the bag on the doormat and left.

Father Michael found the bag when he opened the door a short while later to scatter crusts from his toast for the birds. His eyebrows knit as he picked it up and unwrapped the tape around it. Inside was a jar of homemade jam with a label on it that said: Plum. The cinder parking lot between the rectory and the school was empty in the dim light, as was the street corner where the church stood. Over the trees, he could just make out plumes of smoke from one of the remaining factories in town. It was cold on the step. He looked around for another long moment, then went back inside, closing the door behind him.

Before Mass that next Sunday morning, Doris walked down to the corner diner, went inside, and took her usual stool at the counter. She kept her long, green coat and scarf on, but removed her cap and put it in her lap. Sarah brought Doris her tea with the bag already in the steaming water.

"Thank you," Doris said.

Sarah smiled and thought, as she often did, that Doris looked much the same as she had when she'd been her fifth grade teacher at the Catholic elementary school twenty years before. She had gained weight, of course, but her face held the same kind, tender weariness. Sarah had not known Doris before her son died, so that frame of reference wasn't available to her.

A number of other people sat at the booths and counter. Sarah went around to them with a decanter of coffee. Doris stirred the tea bag, then took it out of the cup and set it in the saucer. She lifted the cup and sipped from it. She could hear the grill spitting in the kitchen. A man laughed at one of the booths, then coughed.

Doris drank her tea until Sarah brought her soft-boiled egg over and refilled her cup with hot water. "You know," Doris said, "there was a time when you couldn't eat before Mass if you were taking Holy Communion."

Sarah nodded. "I remember you telling us that in class."

"Up to an hour beforehand." Doris tapped the shell on her egg with a spoon. "That was long ago now."

Sarah nodded again and went through the swinging doors into the kitchen.

The church wasn't very crowded for that first service. The congregation had gradually declined over the years with most of the factories closing and people moving away. Doris was in her customary pew near the votive candles. Father Michael said Mass in the purple vestments of Lent, murmuring quickly through the prayers while the parishioners did the same.

When it came time for communion, Doris kept her hands folded and took the host from him in the traditional way on her tongue. But she kept her eyes open as she did in order to look at him. What reminded her so much of her son, Dan, wasn't so much his age or the sandy color of his hair or his glasses. It was the vulnerability in his eyes, the slight uncertainty there, the innocence. She could see it best up close like that, and her heart clenched.

It was almost noon when the second Mass ended and Father Michael finished visiting with parishioners on the church steps. He returned to the sacristy and changed from his vestments to his blue shirt, gray trousers, and Mackinaw jacket. He regarded himself in the little mirror on the back of the closet door; he adjusted his glasses and pushed his hair off his forehead.

"A plain young man," he said to himself, "who could

have just as easily been an accountant or someone who repairs watches."

Father Michael took the lunch he'd packed, walked to the rectory's garage, got in his car, and began the drive to his hometown seventy miles away. The day was still gray and he turned the heater on low against the cold. He fiddled with a few stations on the radio, then turned it off.

He ate and watched the telephone wires make their long, rhythmic dip at the edge of the empty fields that were crusted with the late remains of snow. In that part of Ohio, spring's slow entry was still several weeks away.

He stopped at a grocery store at the outskirts of town and bought purple tulips, then made his way out to the cemetery along the river. He drove down one of the gravel lanes, parked under a bare tree, and walked over to his mother's grave, which was perched alone near the river's edge. If his father was alive or buried somewhere else, he had no way of knowing; his father had left when he was very young and he had no knowledge or memory of the man at all.

Father Michael leaned the flowers against the gravestone, clasped his hands, and said a few prayers. Afterwards, he stood listening to the river running fast with melt-off. Grass had not yet grown back to the base of the gravestone; it had only been the previous fall that his mother had died, and then the winter had come on early. A bird called and he watched it lift from a high branch of the tree and fly away over the river, over the empty fields, and into the gray distance.

A cold breeze blew off the river, and with its chill, Father Michael acknowledged that his calling had somehow faded since his mother's death. He wasn't sure exactly why. It was true that he had entered the seminary during high school largely at her urging and that he'd reveled in the pride he knew she felt at his ordination. But he hadn't questioned his convictions before she died, not that he could recall. A train went by at the back of the fields on the other side of the river, a long freight. Once it had passed, it was quiet again.

After Mass, Doris took a walk, stopped for a hamburger, then went to the movies. It didn't matter to her what was playing, and she always sat through the show twice. That way it was already late afternoon when she got home, light had begun to fall, and the day was close to finishing.

She lived in an apartment above a garage and across from a small park. After she let herself in, she looked through the kitchen window and saw the same young family down in the park who had come each day for the past few weeks: a father, a mother, and a girl around eight or nine years of age. The father had tied up the same rope between two trees about ten yards apart. The rope had elasticity to it and intricate loops at the ends, so appeared to have been specially purchased; it was suspended about two feet from the ground. They took turns trying to balance on the rope, and each of them had a distinctive way of attempting to climb up on it. The father's was slow, plodding, and deliberate. The mother's approach was

graceful; she held her hands above her head like a ballerina. The girl simply walked up to the rope and stepped onto it as if she was starting up a set of stairs. The mother or father always held a stopwatch while each of them took their turns. Doris couldn't hear them, but when an attempt was completed, it appeared that the time involved was called out, and there was usually clapping and laughter. The girl was best at it and received the most applause. Since Doris had first seen them, the longest she'd watched one of them manage to stay balanced on the rope was perhaps fifteen seconds, and she hadn't noticed much improvement over time. Still, the family had been coming regularly every afternoon and often stayed for more than an hour. To Doris, they seemed delighted to be together sharing the peculiar activity.

A cold breeze blew off the river, and with its chill, Father Michael acknowledged that his calling had somehow faded since his mother's death.

That afternoon, a thermos had been brought along and the family held Styrofoam cups close to their mouths while they waited their turns. Doris supposed the cups held hot chocolate. Short cloud blasts came off the cups and from their breath. In the gloaming, a streetlamp lit their little arena with a circle of yellow light. Doris put her hand to her chest watching.

Father Michael stopped at a tavern in a refurbished area of a large city he passed through on his way back. It was a neighborhood he knew was regarded for its artistic culture and diversity. The place was dimly lit and practically empty. He took a stool at the L-shaped bar and ordered a draft beer. Acoustic music played softly. He looked at himself in the mirrored wall lined with bottles across from him, smoothed his hair, and blinked several times. The bartender brought his beer over, set it on a coaster, took money, and went away.

Father Michael took a sip of beer and looked around. A group of slightly older men were playing pool at the back, another pair huddled together talking at a table by the window, and a young man about his age sat at the other end of the bar with a beer of his own staring at him. Father Michael met his gaze for a moment, blinked some more, and turned away. He felt blood rising up the back of his neck in a way that was urgent, unsettling, but not unpleasant.

A moment later, the young man was at his side. Their eyes met in the mirror. He asked, "May I sit down?"

Father Michael waited several seconds before gesturing with his hand to the empty stool next to him. The young man sat and they kept their eyes on one another in the mirror, until Father Michael looked down at his glass, turned it in his hand, then lifted it unsteadily to his lips and drank from it.

"My name is Glenn," the young man said. His voice was soft.

"Glenn?" Father Michael heard himself say. They were looking at each other again in the mirror.

"Yes. And you?"

He paused again before saying, "Michael."

"I have a brother named Michael. Younger. And also an uncle, a mentor of sorts, an early supporter."

Father Michael nodded.

The young man said, "So, as you can tell, I'm fond of that name. It has significance. It's a good name." He raised his own glass in salute in the mirror. Father Michael repeated the motion and they both drank. As he did, Father Michael remembered another boy at the seminary and felt something thrilling and electric in the bottoms of his feet. He swallowed hard against it. He thought of his mother and the last rites he'd read her. He stood up suddenly, turned, and walked to the door.

"Hey," he heard the young man say.

But then Father Michael was back outside in the cold, gray mid-afternoon. For a moment, he couldn't remember where he'd parked, then saw his car up the street along the curb, and started jogging towards it, his hands balled into fists in his jacket pockets.

For dinner, Doris heated pea soup on the stove. She ate it from the pan, standing at the counter, looking out the kitchen window at the park. The family had gone home some time ago and full darkness had fallen. The globe of yellow light that had lit the family had widened and touched the edges of the playground where Doris could see the swing set Dan used to love. They'd gone over almost every day after she returned from school. He would squeal with laughter when she pretended that he'd knocked her down, pumping his legs towards her on the swing. He'd been only five when he passed. He'd never inquired about his father; he'd never even asked if he had one.

Doris rinsed the pan and left it in the sink. She picked up the photograph of her son from the kitchen counter and looked at it. In it, she was kissing the side of his head while he smiled; someone had taken it at a birthday party and he wore a pointy hat. She ran her finger slowly across the glass. The frame's gilt had grown tarnished over the years. She replaced it on the counter, opened a cupboard, took out the bottle of rye whiskey, and filled a tea cup with it. She took a sip and carried it into the living room.

Doris turned on the stand-up lamp next to the couch and sat down. She set the cup on the coffee table and began sorting through the pieces of a jigsaw puzzle she'd arranged in groups there. Ten years earlier, before she'd retired, she would have been grading papers and lesson planning at that hour. She worked on the puzzle and sipped from the cup. The only

things that interrupted the silence were a dog who barked a couple of times and a siren that wound its way across town, but she was only vaguely aware of either.

Father Michael didn't sleep much that night. He rose very early, made coffee, and sat at the kitchen table drinking it and looking at his hands. Every now and then a car went by in the street; otherwise, it was quiet. At one point, a small rustling sound came from the front of the house and he turned his head towards it. He walked guardedly to the door, eased it open, and found another paper bag at his feet on the front step. He looked up and down the street and thought he saw the figure of a plump woman turn the corner next to the church, but in the darkness, he wasn't sure. He hurried out onto the sidewalk where he could see past the corner, but aside from a bus pulling away from a stop, the street appeared empty.

Father Michael returned to the front step and picked up the paper bag, which was warm to the touch. He carried it back to the kitchen. It was taped together like the first. He unwrapped it and took out a cellophane package of scones. Their aroma filled the room, and he was reminded of his mother. He set the scones next to his coffee cup and shook his head. It was clear that the scones were freshly baked; whoever made them had to have started the process in the middle of the night. A whistle blew across town at one of the factories. Father Michael reached over to the counter and brought a knife and the jar of plum jam to the table. He unsealed the jar, took one of the scones from the cellophane and sliced it in half.

The diner wasn't very crowded that early on a weekday morning, and except for a mother and her young son at the opposite end, Doris had the counter to herself. She had finished her egg, paid, and was lingering over her tea. She sat watching the boy who was coloring with crayons in a coloring book while his mother read the newspaper.

When Sarah came to take her dishes away, Doris said, "My son used to like to do that."

Sarah followed the older women's eyes and asked, "Color?"

Doris nodded.

Sarah had a son of her own about the same age. She looked back to Doris and said,

"Tell me a little about him."

"Oh," she blew out a breath. "He was a good one, he was. Just so sweet-hearted. Gentle. He was special."

They both looked at the boy at the end of the counter whose brow was furrowed in concentration.

Sarah turned back and said, "And you still miss him."

Doris nodded. "I do. Very much."

Sarah put her hand over her old teacher's on the counter and squeezed it, then took her dishes back into the kitchen. Doris could hear water being sprayed over them.

Confession took place each week at the church on Friday afternoons from three to five. Very few people came, so Father Michael was left mostly to his own thoughts in the dimness of the tiny vestibule. He tried to pray or read scripture, but his mind often wandered.

That Friday afternoon, a cold wind blew rain, so there were even fewer parishioners than normal. Two came during the first hour and none during the second until he was gathering his things together to leave and heard the curtain rustle on the other side. The knee rest groaned under someone's weight. He recognized Doris in her coat and scarf through the screen, and he turned his ear to her as she began, "Bless me, Father, for I have sinned . . ."

> "And I've also been secretive."
> Her voice fell. "I've been
> secretive and snuck about."

Her confession was an ordinary one for her – some unkind thoughts, she'd sworn under her breath at someone lingering in line in front of her at the bank, she'd run through a traffic light. When she paused, Father Michael was readying his usual penance for her of several prayers, but then she said, "And I've also been secretive." Her voice fell. "I've been secretive and snuck about."

"Why?"

"To fulfill my own desires." The old woman's voice was almost a whisper. "Long-held and selfish ones."

Father Michael felt his heart quicken. He said, "I see."

He watched her nod. Blurred through the screen, she could see his eyes, those eyes. They were both quiet while rain was blown against the stained glass windows of the big, empty church.

Finally, Father Michael said, "We all have secret desires, Doris. I do myself. We're all human. That's not a sin."

"Thank you, Father," Doris said. She watched him blinking behind his glasses and wished she could reach through the screen and take his face into her hands the way she had Dan's when he was troubled. "The truth, Father," she blurted, "is that I lost my son many years ago and you remind me of

him. Very distinctly and fondly. I'd like to cook a meal for you. This is what I'd like to do. More than anything."

He gazed intently at her through the screen while the items that had been left on his front step clarified themselves in his mind. He thought of his mother and his lower lip began to quiver.

"All right." His own voice came hushed. "That can be your penance then."

"It won't be a penance, Father. It will be a joy." She paused. "Would tomorrow evening be all right?"

He said, "Yes, fine."

They set a time and she told him where she lived. "It's just across from that little park, from the back of it."

"I know the place," he said. "It's very nice of you to do this. To do these things."

Her hands were folded into steeples in front of her lips. She kissed her fingertips and extended them towards the screen. When she stood, the cushion on the kneeler sighed. He watched her leave through the curtain, heard her steps echo off towards the front of the church, heard the tall doors open and close. Then it was silent again except for the rain.

That next late afternoon was dry and had warmed enough to hint of spring. Father Michael walked over to Doris' apartment along the cracked sidewalks and came through the park. He stopped at the edge of the playground. The same family was arranged around the two trees with the rope strung between. A puzzled frown creased his forehead as he watched them take turns trying to balance on the rope.

Doris stood at her kitchen window watching, as well. The kitchen was full of the good smell of pot roast, potatoes, and vegetables warming together in the oven. She'd added a splash of red wine and was sipping from a juice glass of it as she looked out the window. She saw Father Michael where he stood at the side of the swing set watching and holding a bouquet of flowers. Light was falling, but the streetlamps had not yet come on. Father Michael looked up and their eyes met. She smiled and he smiled back. He made a small wave and she did the same.

Kathleen Hellen

Color Everywhere

As far as I can tell
it's all catastrophe. Indigo stretching
toward brinded night. The frogs' libretto, tires' surf
drenching the weight I carry

on my shoulder like a purse. Nothing beyond
the thwarted light. I envy houses,
as if behind the painted shutters there were

answers. The painted sun
a gold medallion and color everywhere

but where I am, headed for the dwelling
I sometimes confuse for a bank. A woman in a lot,
a woman in a beat-up car the color of an eggplant,
shouts, *Look behind you.* As far as I can tell

the woman hails me like Macbeth. She crows to end-of-world,
Look behind you . . . . Across the sky a band of light. The chance
of orange-yellow-pink in broth. A brushstroke.

Complexity

Lucas Woolfolk
photograph

River Trail

Randall D. Williams
photograph

Elaine Erickson

Des Moines Botanical Garden

This could be Eden –
deep purple shadows, the air filled
with rhododendrons. The sun's halo
rises past slanted windows.
Leaves glide through the dark
side of a mirror.

Some people who wander
down meandering paths
bring with them a broken heart.
Even the fish – red, gold
strands, a dazzling necklace –
somewhere inside them
death lurks as they bleed
from the water's mouth.

Still, it is like strolling
into another life, past wardrobes
of marigolds. Strange strings
tune up, angels rising
out of silken depths to meet
sunlight that astonishes the leaves.

Outside, the rest of the world
rushes by like a fast-moving train,
this garden nestled in a world

gone bad, where freeways,
shopping malls spread like gossip,
cars racing with the river's cold current.

Here a chickadee starts up
from a castle of ferns.

PRV9

Thomas Prinz
mixed media collage

Rustin Larson

Induced

Mozart reaches for the clavier's keys.
   I have one apple in my backpack.
      The light changes. I cross the street,

A few flakes fall from the sky.
   I will spend part of the morning walking.
      I have no money in my pocket.

The waiter brings coffee
   To a table as I pass the café.
      The courthouse tower rings eleven.

A prisoner in an orange jumpsuit
   Is led to the Sheriff's car.
      I keep walking. I reach the park

That has the memorial rock.
   The rock says volunteers drilled here
      Before joining Lincoln's army in the war

Of the rebellion. A long train
   Of heaping coal cars speeds east.
      Each mound of coal is dusted

With snow from further west.
   I saw that clavier, once, when I was thirteen,
      Touring Salzburg. It was in a room

Faintly illuminated for mood.
   It was silent. We were to imagine
      The music. The portrait of Leopold

Frowned down upon us.
   Out in the streets, venders were selling
      Various things to eat. The sky

Was heavy with clouds, and it was
   Late in the afternoon. I bought
      A bag of roasted chestnuts. I had never

Eaten chestnuts before and thought
   They were odd, potatoey and bland.
      The air was misty and cold.

I was becoming sick with a virus.
   As music crosses the ocean, the music
      Can do anything it wants.

When I was four, I was no prodigy or savant.
   I played no keyboard except for the old
      Remington typewriter my mother kept

In the closet. She'd let me roll
   a sheet of lined notebook bond,
      And I would strike the keys,

Being particularly fond
   Of the asterisk
      And it's crisp starlight

Smack against the paper.
Who are you? Who are we? They ask.

Barefoot by Roadkill

Karen J. Weyant

In one version of this memory, I am alone, walking on a road not far from my grandmother's farm. I'm about five years old. It's early spring, and apparitions of asters haunt me. Goldenrod stems splinter and bulge with insects. Skunk cabbages curl in the shade. I am barefoot against my mother's wishes; she had warned me that in spite of the warm spell, it was way too early to go without shoes.

In another version, I'm with my best friend. We are not yet eight years old, skipping along a road by her home in the country. It's late November, and fall grips the air tightly, with a few trees still clutching their dry leaves. A red-winged blackbird scolds us, its scratchy call breaking an otherwise still afternoon.

I don't know why the versions are so different, why I am alone in one memory but with a friend in another, why I remember a cranky bird's call in one recollection while the other holds the signs of spring.

Still, in both versions, there is one image that is the same: someplace along the walk, I see a deer tangled in the guardrails, head flipped forward, chin pushed ahead, forehead scalped with two spots of dried blood.

Near the deer's body, footprints are splattered through the roadside gravel. Someone has stopped to peel the antlers away with the help of a pocket knife. I see the dull outline of a Sears Diehard boot imprinted in the white fur, evidence of a brace and a hard pull. Cheating, some would say, all sense of fair play lost in the clatter and echo of antlers thrown into the bed of a pickup truck, in the chortled backfire and a blue cloud of exhaust smoke, in a prized rack mounted above a fireplace or near a gun cabinet.

Growing up in a small Pennsylvania town cradled by dirt roads and woods, I had seen plenty of roadkill, all rough, mangled mounds of fur or feathers. White-tailed deer were always the most distinguishable, their bodies crumpled in roadside gravel, legs bent and turned in the air like some sort of maneuvers we tried when we played Twister at home.

I knew that hitting an animal was a mistake, an action that was to be avoided, but sometimes, something that couldn't be helped. But the dead were to be left alone.

I looked at the body in front of me. Even in death, the deer would have been beautiful without the desecration. Except for the bloody spots and the single gray footprint, no other injury marked its body, the soft brown fur the same shade as sawdust, the white belly clean as new bed sheets or fresh snow. The eyes were wide open, but the sunlight added a glint to the black pupils. The deer never looked like it had been in pain before it died, only surprised.

Jill Sisson Quinn, in her book, *Deranged: Finding a Sense of Place in the Landscape and in the Lifespan*, recounts her first experience with the dead. She and her sisters had buried their dead hermit crab in the backyard. At seven, being curious about death, she went to the burial place to dig the crab up, cradling its shelled body in her hands. Her sisters found her and, appalled at the sight, threatened her with stories of crab spirits and vengeance. It was in this moment, Quinn explains, "I suddenly realized that I had committed something worse than murder. To kill is sometimes unethical, and sometimes not, but to play with the dead is always perverse."

I, too, learned early to have respect for the dead. While I was growing up, I was surrounded by dead things: baby birds splattered on streets and sidewalks, back porch presents from our cats in the form of field mice or voles, the kill from hunting season strung up in the chilly garage or tied to the backs of my brothers' trucks. The dead were respected: my mother scooped up the birds that crashed into our windows and buried them, while my father taught us to not make fun of the deer that were dangling in the garage. *They lost their lives to feed us*, he said.

His sobering speech led me to my bedroom to gaze at the two skulls nestled in my bottom drawer between tissue paper. One was the skull of a squirrel – I was almost sure. With front teeth dangling like fangs and a round snout, I could almost see the red bandit scolding us from the trees in front of our home. The other skull smaller than my fingertips, was a bird, its beak pointed and sharp, eyes hollow. Sometimes, I thought their spirits haunted me in my dreams, but I didn't get rid of the skulls. They had a better resting spot with my socks and cotton underwear than in the cold ground outside.

The dead also haunted one of my favorite play spots. We

would cut across a field bordering the west end of town to get to Benjie's Bakery – a favorite hangout for the neighborhood kids because the owners had the best ice cream cones: scoops piled high on huge cones for a mere 50 cents. The shortcut was great – it enabled us to get to our favorite spot fast, avoiding the trips north on Ash Street (too long of a walk) or south across West Main Street (too many bars, too much traffic – in that order). We also used the field for a makeshift playground, playing baseball, touch football, and tag. It was a natural part of our summer vacation.

Until the day that my brother told us that our field used to be a cemetery. As proof, he led a group of us kids to a small plot behind a church located on the northern part of the field. In the tangled weeds lay pieces of broken gravestone, the white marble parts crumbling so much that it was impossible to make out names or dates. We also found a small lamb and two broken angels – more proof of a past we did not know existed until that moment.

That year, the movie *Poltergeist* had made its way to HBO, and even if all of us hadn't seen it, we knew the plot line: a family, having moved into a housing development that had been built over an old cemetery, became terrorized by poltergeists that took the youngest girl to their side of the world via television. Sounds silly by today's standards of many horror movies, but it scared us so much that we stayed away from that part of the field. When I did venture back, I tried to push the broken pieces together. Then, I took the lamb, its crouched body that once wore etched swirls for fur but was now smooth, home with me. Still basically intact, the only part that was missing was an ear. I placed the small marble piece in my dresser drawer with my two skulls, sure I could find something that would replace the missing ear.

I never did.

I am still haunted by the dead. I commute 30 minutes to my job through the northern Alleghenies, on a road that is littered with roadkill. Sometimes, someone took time to throw the body of a deer into a drainage ditch or a farmer's field. But it's also not unusual for drivers to find themselves jerking their steering wheels to the side, cars swerving to avoid bloated bodies that are often big enough to cause damage to a vehicle. For some reason, I always want to identify the remains. A round mound of pointy spikes prickling the air is a porcupine, while a narrower body with a bushy tail is a raccoon. Smaller animals, like squirrels and chipmunks, are mere splotches on the road, while birds are easier to identify with their feathers splayed in the air like fans.

Anthony, my partner of seventeen years, says he barely notices the dead. *It's just part of the landscape,* he says. Even when a fresh kill lays splattered, with red streaks of blood soaked into the pavement, he barely makes note of its presence. The only times he says anything at all is when we see the telltale sign of a skunk – black fur spiked with a white stripe. *Roll up your window,* he tells me, *before the smell stinks up the car.*

Roadkill, I once pointed out to him, helps mark the seasons. Bodies blend in with thick piles of plowed snow in the winter while in the summer, the skin and body organs turn to decay faster, black rotting flesh is devoured by maggots. In spring, hoarfrost coats the fur as if the white glaze is a burial shroud. *It's somehow beautiful,* I said to Anthony, who frowned and then admitted that he didn't see anything remotely pleasing about dead animals.

I have had many years of practice with finding beauty in things that many would never notice. While I was growing up, the creeks near my home were not polluted with acid mine drainage; they merely flowed with bright red and orange rusty waves that were the same color as a summer sunset. The deserted factories that lined the edge of town were not ugly, dark skeletons that were reminders of better times. Instead, they contained histories and stories that longed to be told with every creak of rusty doors and crack of weathered window panes. And the old strip mines near my friend's house were not ugly, barren lands – they were mini deserts where small sprigs of plant life could poke their way through and reach for the sun.

As a child, these observations came easily. As an adult, I have to struggle a bit more with defining what is beautiful.

One morning on the way to work, I drove through a thin fog – the kind of fog that does not mask the road, only softens the edges. Still, I am alert, the reflectors on road signs could be the eyes of a coyote, and curled tread from a blown tire could be a raccoon. It's in this way that I saw the beheaded deer.

I thought of the dead deer with the scalped forehead I saw so long ago. Did someone take the head for the prized antlers? I soon found out the answer. Two miles up the road, impaled on a speed limit sign, was the head of the deer, neatly shorn at the neck, antlers still intact, its glassy eyes opened and staring.

I turned my head away, focusing on the road ahead. I didn't tell anyone what I saw.

The next day, the body was gone. Further up the road, the sign and deer's head were also gone. I don't know who removed all the parts.

Whatever teen prank or play I had witnessed was perverse. There was nothing beautiful about a headless body or a deer's head impaled on a road sign. Some could argue, I suppose, that it's no worse than mounted deer heads on living room walls. Still, there is some craft in a taxidermist's hands, some love or care in the work of preserving the dead with sawdust, needles, and thread. What I had seen that day was only brutality.

When I was a child, I saw beauty in the memory – whichever version of the memory it was – of the dead, antlerless deer. I remember standing still, staring, watching the matted fur near the deer's tail curl, like leaves that turn in the presence of a storm. *Soon,* every strand had seemed to murmur, *it's going to rain.* In one version of my memory, my friend had grasped my hand; in the other version, I had cupped my hands together, and because I was the product of rural Pennsylvania's Vacation Bible School programs, I am sure that my palms formed some sort of prayer. And the only thing, really, getting in the way of prayer now, is the steering wheel.

40-Year-Old Male Seeking . . .

Michael Frizzell
oil on canvas

Rob Cook

Because I Could Not Locate
The Mountains He Lost,

I no longer speak to the iambic hermit I was.
How long it took to realize
the meaning of the corn steppes
when they darken toward the movies of Iowa.
I was sick three times,
and then I was healthy four times,
(and I knew the herds of water towers were watching).
It was the Sunday I could hear how deeply
the rain had been searched.
(Because sometimes the children tease
dandelions and do not return.)
Someone said they hunt and kill
even the strongest poems in Iowa.
It was Sunday and the singing of a Rottweiler
stayed trapped inside a scattered child
safe in a circle of warm kennel artillery.
It was Sunday on only one dandelion and it did not return.

Dennis Trudell

A December

The silence of falling snow upon
fallen snow is the song of everyone
who ever lived and died. It will be
my song here in future Wisconsin
nights as flakes briefly glow from
streetlights and farm yard lights.
Men and women will leave beds
to stand in robes watching as our
song surrounds them again and their
hearts move them another snowfall
closer to joining it. The large ears
of deer will hear the snow upon
snow as more than silence, so they
won't hear the song. Yet it will
fill the tracks behind them while it
deepens the inches on roofs above
sleeping children the song is about,
as it is about fawns and journeys
and love and fear and thirst and
temples and everything else. It
can be heard, of course, in other
seasons and climates, the song:
but I am where I am now, and my
parents died within a mile of here.

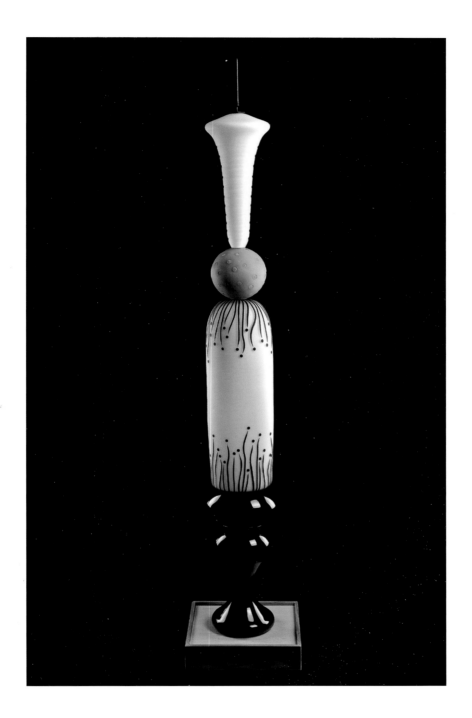

Meadow

Corey Broman
blown, sand-carved, wheel-cut glass, steel, and wood

Hot Head
_____

Christopher A. Meyer
cast iron

Gaylord Brewer

Iguana

A hard lesson to accept:
    That the wild blessing will appear
        only when you cease
            to hunt it, only when effort

is abandoned and, vanquished,
    you are thinking other thoughts:
        of home, perhaps, or a regret
            unforgiven. I am outside my door,

taking therapy of heat and wind.
    Five hot hours by bus, brutal
        trekking of jungle and beach
            in search of the great lizard. Nothing.

Now returned, I look up from reverie
    and it is posed for appraisal,
        emerged from iron bars of grating,
            armor gleaming in the sun.

Fleshy neck extended and an eye
    turned to me. Reader, you doubt
        my conceit, the drum lately
            sounded, that if I sit humbly

the world will come and look?
    We consider each other, patient,
        testing. I feel the old happiness,
            chase the beast into retreat and return

to my chair. Moments later,
    a reptilian head reappears
        above bars, huge crooked claws emerge,
            serrated ridge of thick tail.

We do this again, and again,
    pass hours in parry and play.
        I tell you, my squamous friend
            had no wish to be elsewhere,

that it needed some company
    this lonely holiday morning.
        I tell you it couldn't get enough
            of my monstrous, alien beauty.

Jenna Le

The Twelve Dancing Princesses (IV)

He thinks that I'm untouched, this kingly man
who sits his haunches on the cushioned seat
at the table's head and doesn't speak, this man
who doesn't look a year past thirty-eight

except at those rare moments when I startle
him rising from a nap in the TV room
and, settling dark-rimmed glasses on his turtle-
flat nose, he looks fat-paunched and sixty-two.

He thinks that I'm a virgin, unaware
that I, his kid, who just turned seventeen,
sneak off to tango nightly with strange men

in a magic palace. . . All right, that part's a fib.
But, in the backseat of a fogged-up car,
I've let a boy's ice fingers trace my ribs.

William Jolliff

The Elegance of Seed

The way ground rolled beneath the silver plow,
that ever-slight turning of a brown thigh:
It said, *Here's where the seed goes, right here,*
and here — it can always be just like this.

So we put in the seed. The green machines
rolled their pilgrimage of prairie sea, and
we received the tender indulgence of rain.
We planted old life, and the new life came.

Harlow would say, "They're all just love songs,"
and we sang ours, each pass of the plow,
the disc, the harrow, the drag and the drill.
Then time, and the nervous scratch for sprouts.

By such a faith we live and we will die,
and find in both the elegance of the seed,
the life of all who are born into the world
and come to rest in this fellowship of soil.

Jesse Wallis

Art Imitates Death

Two days before her heart stopped and she fell outside
the front door – keys and the day's mail dropping away
from her clenched hands – Mother had spent a November
afternoon in her eighty-first year at home making pictures
with her ten-year-old granddaughter. The mail was junk.
A crumpled circular of coupons she may well have clipped
out and passed along to any and all. But her last two letters
were *A* and *I*. Going through her things, we discovered them
in the big children's drawing pad leaning against the living
room wall, behind the Minnie Mouse stool, long outgrown.
"*A* is for Angel." She stands in the middle of the blue word,
her gown in white egg tempera on white paper, silver glitter
shimmering on her body, her wings veined like a butterfly's
in a wide checkerboard of black brushstrokes. She is leaning
to the right, one foot higher than the other, wings pointed up,
as if just taking flight. Both hands are empty, closed in pink
fists of concentration, eyes shut in little semicircles of smiles
above a grin the width of her round face. And finally, painted
under this divine messenger, on the next page, "*I* is for Indian
Boy," who stands straight up between the words. Golden feet
firm atop a swirling, thick-brushed river of deep brown earth,
he stares straight ahead, wide-eyed, his hands open and empty.
Green glitter in his wampum belt, red-feathered war bonnet on
black braids. Boy who stands for us, the living, lone and brave.

Introductions

Larry Roots
acrylic on canvas

Clean and Stupid

Joyce Hinnefeld

In recent years I've become almost nostalgic for dirt. Muddy shoes, a whiff of b.o., unwashed hair, an unswept floor. A crumbling house that's gradually succumbing to a riot of overgrown grass and weeds. Maybe I'm just tired, worn out by all the time I've spent trying (and generally failing) to keep myself, and my daughter, and my house, and my yard, up to some unreasonable standard of tidy perfection. Maybe it's both an unreasonable and a mythical standard; maybe it's all in my head. But I don't think so.

In the annals of American history, we have John Wesley's "Cleanliness is next to Godliness," cleanliness as tenth on Benjamin Franklins' list of thirteen "Virtues," and Depression- and Dustbowl-era photographs of poor and dirty Americans. When I was a student at a small college in the Midwest, I recall my mother chastising me for displaying one of the old black and white photos I'd framed and brought from home. It was an image of my oldest brother and a cousin as toddlers, playing in the dirt of the barn lot behind my grandparents' house; my grandmother, in a clean but worn dress and apron, towers over them, Grant Wood-style. "It looks like you're from Appalachia," my mother said, clearly embarrassed that my college friends were seeing this image of not my, but *her*, past – a past that included dirt and suggested poverty.

I teach college students, and it's surprised me, over the last few years, to hear them use the word *hippie* as a term of mild disapprobation. Not an insult exactly; there tends to be an undercurrent of humor, even affection, when they use the term. I've also heard the occasional sneering reference to *dirty hippies*. To be fair, my students have tended to speak more of hippies than of dirty hippies, and they sound almost embarrassed when they use the word. *Real* hippies, they know, are, or were, the age of their grandparents. But in recent years there has been this other thing, this long-haired, tree-hugging, pot-smoking vegan in unfashionable clothes, maybe with dreadlocks, showing up at Occupy sites and anti-fracking rallies. What he or she stands for is all okay probably, maybe even good, but the whole look is just kind of distasteful to certain of these students. For one thing – and it's a big thing – it's probably been a while, a few days or even longer, since this person has had a shower.

Some people my age, born in the early to mid-1960s and rounding out the years of the Baby Boom, felt disappointed to have missed out on the authentic hippie years – the Summer of Love, Woodstock, all those homegrown hallucinogens. Instead we got disco and the revival of the preppy look, Oxford button-downs and Sperry topsiders and Ronald Reagan as president. As a young teen in the seventies, I listened to Joni Mitchell albums and aspired to be like my older brothers, packing an old Ford Falcon for the long drive west from our home in Indiana and some backpacking in places like the Badlands. Maybe one day I'd go backpacking in a place with an evocative name myself, I thought. The only problem would be my hair. A week without a shower would be very bad for my seventies-style long hair with "feathered" bangs that required a blow dryer and a curling iron (think Farrah Fawcett). I hated even imagining what a stringy mess my hair would be if I went backpacking and couldn't take a daily shower. Maybe I could wear a bandana the whole time, I decided. And maybe I'd be sure not to go backpacking with a guy.

This was a problem I never had to solve, because I never went backpacking in the Badlands, or anywhere else. After college and a year of graduate school I moved to Chicago for two years, and then to New York. This was in the 1980's, before the terms of Richard M. Daley in Chicago or Rudy Giuliani in New York – two mayors known for having "cleaned up" their cities, cracking down on crime and burying their seedier elements under a smooth corporate veneer. People like to moan about the bad old days in those cities, the "Dinkins era" in New York or the years prior to Chicago's second Mayor Daley, when Harold Washington was at the helm. But even though there were things I didn't like about the dirt and grime of both cities in those years (waiting for trains in the sticky, smelly summer heat; dealing with aggressive panhandlers; the stench of uncollected garbage on a hot city street), I loved the fact that both were very clearly *cities*. They were worlds away from the small-town life I'd known until I moved to Chicago, and a big part of what set them apart, what made them true cities in my mind, was the fact that they were *dirty*. They had dusty pigeons and graffiti and stairways to the el train or the subway that reeked of urine. They also had lots of independent bookstores and cheap places to eat and little hardware stores where you could have a key to your apartment made for your boyfriend, and nary a Gap nor a Target, Office Max nor TGI Friday's to be found.

In Chicago I went to cafes and clubs in neighborhoods like Wicker Park and Bucktown, which still felt artsy and edgy and mildly dangerous back then. I rode there on the back of my boyfriend's motorcycle (Who needed backpacking in the Badlands? I *was* bad!). In New York I walked to Astoria Park, near the Triborough Bridge, from my first apartment in Queens. Once I watched an underwater dance performance in the massive Astoria Pool, another time a concert by the strange and wonderful Sun Ra and his Arkestra, and always I saw large and boisterous families having picnics. *I am definitely not in Indiana anymore*, I thought, as I walked by the men seated outside the Greek tavernas on 30th Avenue, drinking their coffee and watching me. A friend that I worked with in Manhattan invited me to a party at her boyfriend's place in Williamsburg, Brooklyn, but some other friends at work – white ones – advised me not to go alone. That's how long ago this was: Williamsburg was not yet the destination neighborhood it would become. No place in Brooklyn was, really, with the exception of Brooklyn Heights, and maybe Park Slope.

I should mention that through the nearly ten years that I lived in both gritty, pre-Richard M. Daley Chicago and dirty, Dinkins-era New York City, I was never the victim of a crime. Except for one time, when my checkbook was lifted from my bag on the subway in New York. (That's also how long ago this was: we wrote checks.) On a day when I'd carelessly thrown the thing in an unzipped pocket and sat down, in a sleep-deprived daze, right next to the door of a very crowded car – something no reasonably rested and conscious New Yorker ever did in those days. There my checkbook sat, right alongside a quick and easy exit, beckoning. *I* might have taken it if it hadn't been mine – and if I hadn't known how little money was actually in the account.

And yet it's not quite accurate, historically, to depict cities as sites of dirt and anarchy.

"In the process of making art," writes Lee Upton in her book *Swallowing the Sea: On Writing and Ambition, Boredom, Purity and Secrecy,* "an idealization of purity may become a bitter antagonist, sternly disallowing much of what is muddled, snarled, and anarchic about being human." It was that muddled, snarled, and anarchic stuff I was after, I think, in moving from small-town Indiana to Chicago and then to New York. And yet it's not quite accurate, historically, to depict cities as sites of dirt and anarchy. As historians Suellen Hoy, author of *Chasing Dirt: The American Pursuit of Cleanliness*, and Kathleen M. Brown, author of *Foul Bodies: Cleanliness in Early America,* both note, *all* Americans – both rural and urban – were initially perceived as filthy in comparison to civilized Europeans. And eventually American cities, with their improved systems for providing water, handling sewage, and preventing disease (thanks to the efforts of organizations like the Municipal Order League in

Chicago, and the Women's Christian Temperance Union and Ladies Health Protection Association in New York), were understood to have far surpassed still-dirty rural America in civility, and cleanliness, and class.

Even the first century stoic philosopher Epictetus connected cleanliness with cities. If you want to be a philosopher, for God's sake take a bath, he advised his pupils – lest you drive people away from philosophy with your unpleasant smell. And if you insist on reveling in your body's natural odors, stick to the countryside. "You think you deserve to have a scent of your own," he is recorded as admonishing his listeners in *The Discourses of Epictetus*:

> *Very well, deserve it: but do you think those who sit by you deserve it too, and those who recline by you, and those who kiss you? Go away then into a wilderness, where you deserve to go, and live by yourself and have your smell to yourself, for it is right that you should enjoy your uncleanness by yourself. But if you are in a city, what sort of a man are you making yourself, to behave so thoughtlessly and inconsiderately?*

I never lost a sense of myself as a child of the rural hinterlands during my years in Chicago and New York. This may explain why, though I was blonde and fair and didn't speak Spanish or Greek or any of the other languages I heard as I walked along the Queens side of the East River in the late 1980's, I felt a greater affinity for the big, noisy families I saw picnicking there than I did for the people I saw during the week, on the sidewalks of midtown Manhattan. "O generation of the thoroughly smug / and thoroughly uncomfortable," writes Ezra Pound in "Salutation" – a brief poem that, when I first read it years ago, reminded me of my earlier walks through Astoria Park – "I have seen fishermen picnicking in the sun, / I have seen them with untidy families, / . . . And I am happier than you are, / And they were happier than I am."

Was I happier than those people in midtown Manhattan? Probably not. I was often lonely and confused about my future; I wanted to be a writer but felt afraid to say so, and I was chronically worried about money. And were those families picnicking by the East River happier than I was? That, of course, is impossible to know, just as it's impossible to say who was cleaner or tidier.

"And the fish swim in the sea / and do not even own clothing," the poem concludes – an inarguable point. Of course the "thoroughly smug" and "thoroughly uncomfortable" generations Pound was addressing in his poem were not clean, well-heeled New Yorkers but, more likely, other poets of his generation, the ones he and T.S. Eliot and H.D. and William Carlos Williams aimed to displace with their imagism and vorticism, their *vers libre*. Still, there's no denying the fact that in the world of "Salutation," the only people who come close to the happy lives of unencumbered fish are those who are "untidy." Surprising, maybe, considering the fact that, as Lee Upton notes, Pound sought a kind of purity in language and poetry, admiring "the fascist 'purifier' Mussolini," and echoing French poet Stéphane Mallarmé, who "sought to 'purify the language of the tribe.'"

Upton's exploration of purity in literature ranges widely, from the hot baths Elizabeth Taylor is purported to have described as virginity-restoring through Pablo Neruda's defense of "impure poetry" and Anne Carson's explorations of women and desire, fluidity and impurity, in Ancient Greece. The female body, like the poor body, is another site of uncleanness; it bleeds, and smells, and produces raging hormones, all the things that lead to greasy hair and blemishes on the skin and various other terrors of my life as a female teenager – my own years ago, and increasingly, these days, those of my teenage daughter.

For all the defenses and explorations of impurity in some writers' work, the lure of purity remains potent in both our language and our literature, Upton knows. It's there in the work of Ezra Pound, as well as that of Emily Dickinson and Sylvia Plath, and in the lingering influence of works like Charles Lamb's "Cleanliness," with its depiction of soil that "Argues a degenerate mind, / Sordid, slothful, ill inclin'd." I like Upton's take on the point-of-view character in Muriel Spark's story "You Should Have Seen the Mess," with her stolid middle-class preference for cleanliness over pleasure or intellect or art. "This hygienic, self-satisfied little person seems perfectly comfortable and benignly confident about her choices," Upton writes. "She's clean, and she's stupid."

My wistful recollection of my younger life in untidy cities – what I've begun to call my nostalgia for dirt – seemed to reach new heights in the winter of 2012, when I attended an academic conference in Chicago. I'd been back a few times before that, but, maybe because I'd stayed with a friend on the northwest side of the city on those previous visits, I hadn't quite taken in the changes downtown, in the Loop, and along Michigan Avenue. The polished chrome, video-screen, Disney/the new Times Square look of so much of it. *Some* things were still the same, I was relieved to see, like the bare, cold, closed-down winter feeling of Grant Park south of Randolph Street, and the dirt and noise of the Wabash Avenue elevated tracks.

On several occasions I met up with people I knew at a Starbucks in the Blackstone Hotel, at the southern end of the Loop, and I told all of them the same story. For a brief period in my early twenties, I worked in the box office of a little theatre that was housed in a ballroom on the lobby level of the Blackstone. When, on this visit to Chicago in 2012, I went in search of that box office, I found that its window had been discreetly paneled over. A potted plant stood in front of it. Back in the 1980s, there'd been an old-fashioned coffee shop one floor down from the lobby, at street level, that was always closed by the time I came to work. I have a vivid memory of sitting on the carpeted stairway outside this closed coffee shop one Saturday evening, waiting for a friend to return from the bathroom in the lobby, and watching through the window as three rats chased each other around the counter stools. That place had become the Starbucks where I now sat chatting with my fellow writers.

Who cares? the friends I met up with in Chicago probably thought – or more likely: did you have to include the part about the rats? But they all humored me. These were writers, after all, people who were comfortable with my nostalgia and

sympathetic to my misgivings about the city's new sleekness and fastidiousness. Its purity. The sidewalk outside the entrance to the main conference hotel was packed with mostly younger writers, many of them probably graduate students, all of them smoking. Each time I walked in or out of the Chicago Hilton's front doors, I passed through a dense cloud of smoke. Through the smell of an old coffee shop or an old bar. Of my own impure youth.

> Everywhere I turn these days, there are antibacterial soaps and ointments, hysteria over Ebola or the next virulent strain of flu.

Now I live in a town that, for reasons I don't fully understand, often smells like clean laundry – olfactory evidence of Suellen Hoy's observation that by the latter half of the twentieth century Americans had become "a people that used more water and had more bathrooms per family than any other nation on Earth." The dryer vents from many of the apartment buildings and college dorms must somehow be directed towards Main Street. When I walk around downtown I smell, not urine or garbage, not even automobile exhaust, but fabric softener.

I see this tidying, hygienic impulse everywhere, even on visits to the Midwestern farm town where I grew up and where, in recent years, the influence of Martha Stewart has been undeniable – trimmed, weed-free lawns and orderly pots of impatiens in front of the houses, old bicycles or sleds artfully arranged beside them. And in the farm fields that surround the town on all sides, ridiculously neat rows of corn and soybeans, grown from genetically modified seeds. Everywhere I turn these days, there are antibacterial soaps and ointments, hysteria over Ebola or the next virulent strain of flu. And behind this hysteria: the shift from seeing our own bodies as potentially contagious to potentially vulnerable that has fueled the anti-vaccination movement, as recounted by Eula Biss in *On Immunity*. The clean and supposedly "natural" twenty-first century body, in need of protection from dirt and bacteria on one side, and from the vagaries of medical science on the other.

"We need germs," Biss reminds us, pointing to immunologist David Strachan's 1989 "hygiene hypothesis," which suggested that our overly sanitized environments could actually be making our children more susceptible to allergies and asthma. At least some measure of people's fears of environmental toxins – and of vaccines – Biss notes, is rooted in notions of personal purity that go back to cultural anxieties about "the evils of the flesh," and about poverty. And purity, she reminds us, is "the seemingly innocent concept behind a number of the most sinister social actions of the past century." For example:

> *A passion for bodily purity drove the eugenics movement that led to the sterilization of women who were blind, black, or*

poor. Concerns for bodily purity were behind miscegenation laws that persisted more than a century after the abolition of slavery, and behind sodomy laws that were only recently declared unconstitutional. Quite a bit of human solidarity has been sacrificed in pursuit of preserving some kind of imagined purity.

I think a lot about my young teenage daughter's efforts to navigate the cleanliness-and-purity gauntlet. That winter when I returned to Chicago, when she was ten, she wasn't yet preoccupied with purity – though at age five, she did announce, with disgust, that the only clean place in all of New York City was the American Girl store. At age ten she was a deep appreciator of dirt and clutter. She preferred to be barefoot at all times. She hated having her nails trimmed and argued vehemently against taking showers. Until recently, she was baffled by my constant urging that she at least make a path through the pile of clothes and books and other unidentifiable things on the floor of her room.

But my daughter is now fourteen, and part of a generation that seems to have at least some things in common with mine, back in the Reagan-era eighties. Sperry topsiders, the preppy shoe of choice during my college years, are back, and my daughters' friends' conversations – like a number of my students' short stories – are littered with brand names (Starbucks, Vineyard Vines, Burberry, Warby Parker, Urban Outfitters). A few years ago, when I drove my daughter and a friend of hers by the local library – where our small but faithful band of Occupy protesters had camped out on the neighboring public plaza – I'm certain I heard the polite, sweet-natured young friend in the back seat mutter, "Get a job."

Possibly the only thing worse than being a dirty hippie in an age of rampant consumerism and corporate-sponsored shaming of physical imperfection is being the mother of an unclean child or the keeper of an unclean house. "To keep the world clean – this is the one great task for women," wrote nineteenth-century home economics lecturer Helen Campbell. At some point when my daughter was younger I became aware that some of my old teenage fears were resurfacing, now focused on her. What would her teachers – or worse: the mothers of her friends – think if I let her go out with her nails looking like that? Should I tell her she really ought to take a shower because her hair (her long, seventies-style hair – sans Farrah Fawcett wings, of course) is starting to look, well, a little *greasy*? "The germ-obsessed twenty-first century mother," writes Kathleen M. Brown in *Foul Bodies*, "has inherited the Victorian mother's responsibility for setting and enforcing standards. Nagging, repeating, and reminding mark her role as civilizer."

At times I hear that nagging, repeating Victorian civilizer voice coming out of my very own mouth, and when I do, I hate its shrill, upper-nasal cavity sound. Friends with older kids used to assure me that soon enough my daughter would want to take several thirty-minute showers a day. Let her find her way to an all-American obsession with cleanliness and purity on her own, they told me – and they were right. With puberty has come daily showers and the familiar worry about less than squeaky-clean hair, or a body that smells like something

other than fruity soap. Just like that she's become a version of me, of the me I recall with a mixture of wistfulness and pain. Obsessively preoccupied with my skin. Embarrassed by the need to head to the bathroom with a tampon or pad.

Here I am, supposedly older and wiser, yet still capable of deep embarrassment about, for instance, the state of my untidy house and yard. But what pre-hygienic American wilderness am I actually remembering, or imagining, as I succumb to this nostalgia for dirt? My hometown, pre-Martha Stewart? The lawns and houses might have been less orderly, but it truly wasn't equivalent to, say, James Agee and Walker Evans' world of Alabama sharecroppers. And the farm fields that I recall as less pristine were, in fact, part and parcel of a monolithic system of factory farming, even when I was a child.

I think there's something else about this particular historical moment that has made me so attuned to our passion for cleanliness, and that is my sense of this as a kind of liminal moment, a sort of holding of our collective breath before exhaling – into what exactly? After Martha Stewart and late twentieth-century excess, after gallon upon gallon of anti-bacterial soap and diseases we can't seem to eradicate, after a stubborn economic downturn that all our gadgets and online shopping and viewing of silly videos can't quite distract us from, what comes next?

I had a profound sense of this liminal moment in the fall of 2014, when I attended my thirtieth college reunion. The town on the Ohio River near my alma mater has been Martha-ized as well, for years now, and while the restaurants and the coffee are undeniably better, there were things that I missed on that visit. Like the old hotel where, pre-gentrification, my oldest brother and his wife stayed when they came to visit me one December weekend in 1980 (I remember, because it was the weekend after John Lennon was shot). Back in those days that hotel had a single bathroom down the hall and mainly housed long-term residents. But when I returned in the fall of 2014, a friend and I had lunch in an expensive restaurant on the ground floor and learned, from the restaurant's host, about the extensive renovations upstairs. The next morning, walking around the town, I came upon a big brick building I didn't recall, an old cotton mill near the river; the windows were blown out, and torn white curtains fluttered in the breeze. The inside was empty, stripped bare, and on the brick wall beside the padlocked front door was a poster with an invitation to invest in the forthcoming "Riverfront Mill Resort" and a drawing of the planned restoration. The poster was so sun-faded that I could barely make out the words. Later I found a 2009 video depicting the beautiful, sustainably designed restoration plans on YouTube; it had 439 views and one comment: "Will anything ever happen with this glorious old building or will nature reclaim it like it has so many others?"

Which feels like a version of the question I keep asking myself: What's next? What happens once we've rid our bodies and our houses, our fields and our food, everything, of every visible physical flaw? One of the best answers to this question that I've seen is Tina Fey's riff on Photoshop in *Bossypants*: "I don't see a future in which we're all anorexic and suicidal. I do see a future in which we all retouch the bejeezus out of our own pictures at home. Family Christmas cards will just be eyes and nostrils in a snowman border."

Our images of the future, at least as they appear in films and books and other popular media, seem to me to fluctuate between two extremes right now: a sleek, pure, minimalist space-age world (think the latest Apple product) and a dystopian wilderness (smoking and trash-filled in some versions, wildly overgrown and populated with ravenous and possibly genetically mutated beasts in others). My picture of the first version, as I try to imagine it enacted in my own life, looks like this: a clean, white desk with nothing on it but a thin electronic tablet of some kind. The desk I'll presumably never have, because I keep writing things down on pieces of paper and tucking these into random and disorganized files, with the vain hope that all this note-taking will help me keep track of all the things I keep not finishing, or not remembering. In certain moods my desk and my office – like my house, like my yard, like my own body, still, at times – shame me. They're anarchic messes. *You should have seen the mess*, hisses Muriel Spark's stodgy character and other imagined judges in my mind, as I peruse the piles of paper and files, the boxes crammed into corners and under tables.

Or my messy, overgrown yard. Because now, as if it weren't enough to worry about my less than perfectly clean house, there are the beautifully landscaped lawns and gardens of my daughters' friends, generally viewed from the front seat of my car as I'm dropping her off. Or, even worse, the new concept of the "outdoor room": not a yard, not even a mowed and reasonably tended one, but a space that's so pristine, and with such comfortable and attractive furniture, that you can cook, eat, and live there. This has been my most recent experience of feeling inadequate – that is, less than pure – as a mother: my sense that our unkempt yard and crumbling back porch mark me as a kind of failure as an American adult.

Years ago I saw a sign in my neighborhood advertising a lawn care business called "Silent Meadows;" apparently the owners of the company had not heard of Rachel Carson. "Lawns are nature purged of sex and death," wrote Michael Pollan back in 1989 in "Why Mow? The Case Against Lawns;" "no wonder Americans like them so much." Today, though we may have banished DDT from American landscapes, the chemicals we've continued to spray on our perfectly green, perfectly trimmed lawns have had disastrous effects on the ecosystem, diminishing populations of pollinators like honeybees to dangerously low levels.

Yes we need to practice basic personal hygiene. Yes we need clean water and sanitary waste disposal and a means of routing cholera, and yes, as Eula Biss argues forcefully and eloquently, we also need vaccinations. Because we are part of a community, and part of the larger world, and as such, we have certain responsibilities, including making use of our many resources and economic advantages to control contagion and work to eradicate disease. But an obsession with purity is isolating, and can negate that sense of connectedness and responsibility. "We have more microorganisms in our guts than we have cells in our bodies," Biss reminds us – "we are crawling with bacteria and we are full of chemicals. We are, in other words, continuous with everything here on earth. Including, and especially, each other."

So I'm training myself to appreciate my own backyard, to see it as a wonderfully wild outdoor room, one that's been "reclaimed by nature," with as much clover and thistle and Virginia creeper as grass (probably more). There is no plant classification called "weeds," my sister-in-law reminds me every time we talk about gardening; *weed* is just a word for something you don't want. I'm trying to want all of it, or most of it – the native species, at least, and, as my neighbor, the beekeeper, is teaching me to notice, the plants that are beloved by pollinators and birds. And that's the other image of the future I'm calling up lately: wild things growing as they wish, something like that "glorious old building" reclaimed by nature, or the world of so much recent post-apocalyptic fiction. Like the setting of Emily St. John Mandel's novel *Station Eleven*, a middle America, and presumably an entire world, in which electronic gadgets – electricity for that matter – are only a vague memory, and the heroic young woman at the novel's center wields knives, *Hunger Games*-style, with ruthless precision.

> Today, though we may have banished DDT from American landscapes, the chemicals we've continued to spray on our perfectly green, perfectly trimmed lawns have had disastrous effects on the ecosystem . . .

I suppose my growing fondness and nostalgia for dirt seem to point to a preference for this second view of the future, for an old mill that's overtaken by nature, slowly sinking into the earth, rather than a renovated home for stores and condos – nature triumphing over technology, or something vaguely silly like that. But I'm enough of a child of the sixties (I was born then, at least) to long for a different picture than that of the violent, post-apocalyptic worlds of recent American books and films. It's a utopian, rather than dystopian, picture: the image of my daughter in recent summers, deep in the woods at the wonderful, electronics-free, dirty-hippie, Quaker summer camp she attended. Each time we picked her up she was barefoot, in a tie-dyed t-shirt and dusty old shorts – muddy, faintly ripe-smelling, and wielding no *Hunger Games* knives. Also happier, and more placid, than she'd been for months leading up to her time at camp.

But last summer was her last at that camp, until she's older and maybe goes back as a counselor. She also keeps her room pretty tidy now, or at least I think she does. If she doesn't, I don't have many opportunities to nag her about it. The door's generally closed.

Great Sand Dunes

Robert Gillespie
photograph

Christopher Todd Anderson

Twilight

I hold twilight in my lap.
Kittenfur gray, she padded
through the eastern corn field

(fallow now, stalk stubble),
across the unmown lawn
to find me sitting alone

on the brickwork patio;
she curls softly against
my belly: a turbulent day's

only only comfort.
Twilight purrs
her soft underthrum:

pond frogs and crickets,
leaf-sigh, and the dove's
pensive *ah-woo woo woo.*

• • •

Mothercat night stalks
the treeline: feral, hungry.
She believes darkness is her

only daughter, but her belly
swells, pregnant with stars
that will suckle cold

white light. Night the huntress
velvets her claws. There will be,
later, time enough for bad dreams'

puncture wounds, time enough
for the killing bite of loneliness
or the midnight phone call.

Mothernight creeps through
underbrush and leaf litter.
Moons sing their milksongs.

Acceleration

Jenny Bye
encaustic on canvas

M.B. McLatchey

Ocracoke

In a letter to his wife, sure and seasoned,
he said, I will be back. I will cross channels

and oceans and islands and rushing rivers.
And for the rest of her years, his flannel

shirt that she made her own, caught her
tears as they might in a lover's hold.

What are our days, she wrote,
or distances, or promises, or years,

if not one heartbeat measured out
in a country's checkered grid, weave

in a cloth — worn, endeared. As once
in Ocracoke — barrier island, barrier

to all that does not hold against cruel winds
and so, not love, which holds and takes

its fortitude from simpler things: the stillness
that follows cruel words; the kiss that cools

ankle and wrist like a shore bird in low waters;
gestures of a land within a land —

a dress that I saw in a shop and I longed
as we ferried away, as a small girl longs

for sea winds catching its hem in a gust
of sea spray above my knees. And you wanted

to please me because — I would come to see —
that is what lovers do. Let's go back, you said.

And I noticed the difference in miles for me
and you: what for me was a turn in our plans

and a girlish yearning, was for you love's open hand —
a summer dress on a wooden hanger — ocean and sand

that we might reclaim like a sparrow's song
played and replayed. No distances, no time —

I learned that day — no ferry we cannot take
from lover's gift to lover's ache.

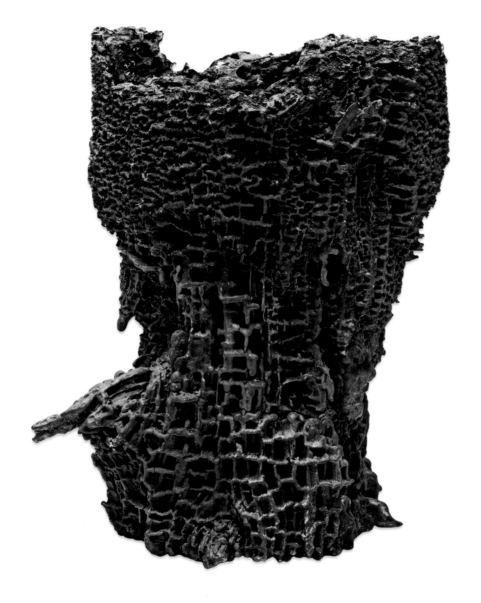

Death Star

Christopher A. Meyer
cast iron

Fusion

Lucas Woolfolk
photograph

Richard Robbins

Bathtub Mary

In our county, porcelain
grottoes float on the lawns – tipped
vertical, planted halfway –
so now the iron-red stripe,

for years our shame when hosting
houseguests, swings up, a comet
tail vaulting Mary's low sky,
one geranium to the next.

And she deals her miracles
even here, simple fields turned
to noise large as the world. We
listen some nights to the corn

and in that absolute dark
hear chairs, our barn, our flat talk
all slide below us as we
rise to the right hand of God.

Jacqueline Sullivan

At the Swimming Pool

All winter I imagine you,
immaculate cube in blue,
confidently asleep inside the sun
of a thousand Saturdays yet to come.

Above, the wind plays tricks
on unsuspecting blackbirds,
dazed they're diving sideways,
apostrophes without the words.

Children shriek and run full speed
with bleached-out towels
around their shoulders,
little super heroes.

A whistle trills.
The lifeguard is unseen.
I never find out what happened
in between.

Novels sit half-opened
in people's laps,
like *Orphan Train*, its company
a weathered book mark.

Duke basketball t-shirt,
lower half drenched,
dries out on a picnic table bench
now back in season.

The diving board
is free for a second.
Jump off, jump off,
go in, before it's cold again.

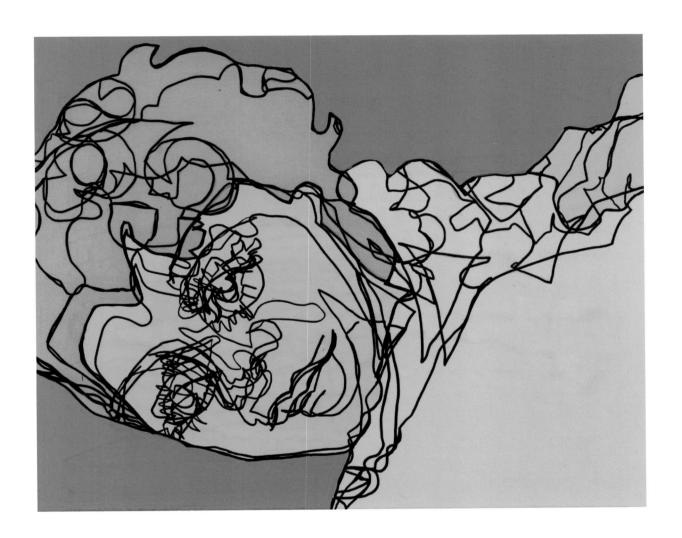

Janet

Jodi Whitlock
mixed media

Christina Seymour

Stage-Struck

1.

Piecing together the loose strings of last night's argument,
I take a step toward belief and end in nature –
the silken bark that moss commits to, the beginning of coping with lost hands.

I create you over and over,
to perfect light behind trees,
unlike the simplicity of construction paper squirrels in a kindergarten class.
Some poets say, *the sea is etched*; my father said, *inspiration is not gone from your life*;

2.

The Van Gogh made a music of my lost temperament: its stringy whites and carpet blues shared that moment of dissonance between us. It said, *I understand you, both of you*, and silence let our claims fall like worn sheets, cotton-frayed, feather-light, and finally the sun receded to make just one mountain visible – the hook-topped one – the godly nose of something immoveable but present. The parting of my lips gives room for two new shiny objects to enter – forgiveness and light.

3.

Near the noontime shine, I unclasped,
cherry blossom dropping opulence near the dusty, lost doll
on the shelf of my memory. Gratitude is the stuffed tiger by her side.

I held your hand as a way of saying,
why must the carousel be a metaphor
for relentlessness?

I held your hand to say, *here we are,*
this imperfect dune on the beach of the rest of our lives,
and it has to be enough.

BR1

Thomas Prinz
mixed media collage

One Stroke/Two Strokes

Karen Chesterman
oil and wax on canvas

Z.G. Tomaszewski

Spectacle

My grandpa came to me in a dream.
Not the sort of dream you would guess
when sleep comes. Instead, the dream
from half awake, standing up, from
the crease between cloud and leaf cover,
in a dream housed among the changing seasons,
the space created by groundswell and rain in hand.

My grandpa came to me through the thickets
of lilacs, stepping over glacier lilies, but
stepping on the litter of twigs and brush
just missing the dens of our small ancestors.

He came with glasses fogged and the moon
above his left shoulder. He came when deer
entered the meadow, while the woods blurred.

He came here with the river in his skin
and a single word, which, though I cannot
be sure, sounded like *stone.*

Because he came half suspended in a misty light
I search for him beyond the stenciled pine,
on the rusted points of barbs from an old fence.
I look for a certain grain of light waving through
the grass and the sound of rocks in a pocket.

Spring gives itself over.
Summer offers a few more flowers.

I take a walk and find his glasses.
I put them on, look out into the haze.

The Space Between

Liv Spikes

I am smoking a Marlboro 100, speeding to the OB-GYN's office saying, "Shit. Shit. Shit." between drags. 100's are those extra-long cigarettes old women playing slot machines and classic Hollywood actresses smoke. I bought a pack of them because Harry, the owner of the liquor store I frequent, forgot to order the regular Marlboro Lights in a box. And given the choice between extra-long telephone pole cigarettes and blue-collar soft packs, I opt for the former. I glance down at the clock, assured I can be out of the doctor's office in time for spin class.

I make a large and frantic entrance into the waiting room and announce, "I was just on the phone with Maryanne and she told me to come here right away because I have really bad cramps, and I'm 13 days late, and my boobs are killing me." A reasonable looking woman reading *Good Housekeeping,* probably waiting for her annual wellness exam, glances up at me, and rolls her eyes. I can see her thought as though it were projected in a cartoon bubble above her head: *Did you ever think to take a home pregnancy test?! Honestly.* It's a reasonable question, and if I'd so much as Googled "early pregnancy symptoms" I would have come up with that on my own. But having never been pregnant before, I have no idea early pregnancy symptoms are exactly the same as horrible PMS.

I am escorted to the restroom by my least favorite, fake nurse tech lady. Techs generally complete an associates program at the community college; they are not health care providers. Fake nurse is wearing Care Bear scrubs. She hands me a small plastic cup and instructs me to slide it through the window when I'm finished.

Having delivered my sample, I return to the nurse's check-in station for blood pressure and temperature checks. The fake nurse opens my file on her little computer and sighs before finding the energy to review my current medications. Midway through the list she pauses, looks at the Petri dish on her counter and says, "Okay, your pregnancy test is negative." I exhale both relief and a sort of *I already knew that* arrogance.

"Oh . . . wait. Positive."

I shoot her a look previously reserved for my mother and anyone at the DMV. I want to punch fake nurse in the face.

Then I start to cry, deep sobs fueled as much by the excess of progesterone as shock. I'm cupping my face with my palms, bawling for what seems like several minutes before fake nurse hops off her stool of authority and puts her hand on my shoulder.

"But you're married, right?" she offers.

I am married. Twenty-eight and a far cry from the knocked-up, Catholic school girl I seemed to be imitating.

I'm still crying with a blood pressure cuff on my arm when fake nurse adds, "And according to the first date of your last period, your due date is September 20th." I squint my already swollen and narrowed eyes at her as if to convey, *You're a horrible, horrible person and no one likes you or your Care Bear scrubs.*

Everyone's initial reaction to that all important color-changing pee stick is different. A wanna-be mama since the age of four, my visceral reaction to the news was the opposite of what I would have expected to feel. I always imagined running out of the bathroom, evidential wand in hand, exclaiming, "We're pregnant!" to my doting husband who would scoop me and twirl me around with glee.

I spent the night we found out I was pregnant crying alone in our guest bed. I felt an instinct to curl into myself, to withdraw in order to process. I didn't want this yet; I wasn't ready. I lay wrapped in blankets of self-pity, exhausted in a hormonal haze thinking, *Fetus, Fetus go away, please come back another day.* I was going to get fat. I was going to lose my edge. I hadn't even assembled our wedding album yet. I liked my clothes, my very small clothes. I was not ready to take the parenthood plunge.

All I wanted to do was drink three glasses of wine, smoke five cigarettes, chase it all with an Ambien, and suddenly, without warning, none of these were options; my front line coping mechanisms had been taken away. And so I lay there – raw, puffy, and unable to shut off my thoughts.

At my first official prenatal visit three days later the doctor congratulated me, and for the first time, it didn't feel uncomfortable. I said, "So I'm really pregnant, there's a little person coming together down there?"

"Well, we don't actually consider it a person yet, but yes. And your progesterone levels are sky high which is a great indicator of a viable pregnancy."

At the checkout desk they gave me a canvas tote filled with magazines and books on pregnancy. The bag was packed with four boxes of prenatal vitamins, and pamphlets on the local hospital's Lamaze classes. Driving away, with my Healthy Pregnancy Kit riding shotgun next to me, I felt a smile creeping across my face, a lightness of spirit. I was pregnant. So it's a little earlier than we'd hoped for… so what?

I drove to Barnes and Noble. I filled my arms with *What to Expect When You're Expecting*, *Your Pregnancy Week by Week*, and *The Pregnancy Diet*. Finally, I picked out a spiral-bound journal with bright jungle animals on the cover.

I wrote dozens of times a day, a sentence here, a paragraph there, ten pages before bed. I knew every thought and feeling I was having was unique and specific to this moment in my life and I didn't want to forget any of it. I wrote endlessly about how tender my giant boobs were, I wrote that if we had a girl, she (unlike her mother) would know how to change a tire and balance a checkbook. I wrote about how much pasta I was eating and how delicious real ice cream was.

Many women describe a feeling of "fullness" early in pregnancy. I would add to that, heaviness and instantaneous "doughy-ness." My breasts filled up like water balloons overnight, my previously defined waist seemed to exhale in one deep sigh. It was uncomfortable, and I knew it was only the beginning. At six weeks pregnant, I packed up my tiny clothes, folding size zeros away, indefinitely. I bought maternity clothes; they didn't fit, but already nothing did. The idea began to grow on me that a real baby-person would soon fill out the stomach panel of these hideous though oddly adorable pants, that a telltale bump would replace the general squishiness that must have been necessary to get my pea-sized embryo off on the right foot. We had gotten what so many couples in our generation never get – a surprise pregnancy. Who was I to bicker over a few months mistiming?

In the first trimester of pregnancy, a weight gain of three to five pounds is typical. By eight weeks, I had gained fourteen. It felt strange that I couldn't do anything about that. With my normal fluctuations, I could restrict, I could exercise for hours on end, dropping weight like a high school wrestler if I wanted to. But for now, for once, it wasn't about me. This was a surprisingly delightful and freeing revelation.

I was headed to the gym for a very light workout one evening, equipped with my double sports bra get-up when my husband said, "Love you, babe. Remember Fe doesn't want your heart rate above 160."

"Fe?"

"Yes, the little fetus growing inside you. Fe. Remember the doctor said to keep it light."

"We got it," I said as I closed the door behind me. We: me and Fe, my new built-in buddy who had come along, it seemed, to save me from myself, to force me away from the cigarettes, the partying, the breakfast of coffee and coffee for lunch meal plan I'd adapted, all of it. On my way into the gym I patted my lower belly reverently and whispered, "Thanks for coming, Fe.

Nature had her chance on this one, and I wasn't going to be screwed by her again.

My husband and I were both ready for our nine week ultrasound. We'd seen the physical changes in me, and now we were ready to have some empirical evidence of Fe. It was time at last to hear her heart beat. The ultrasound tech slid the machine's wand inside me. I looked down at it and wondered how much longer I'd be able to see her hand over my tummy, how strange it would be when I was belly-blocked from everything below my boobs. A dark, bean-shaped image appeared on the screen. She said, "This is the sac." My husband and I exchanged smiles, eyes twinkling. Then the tech's face went a little blank. She seemed to be probing me harder with the wand, more intently. Better at reading facial expressions than fuzzy ultrasound images, I said, "Now what about the heartbeat?" and she said, "I can't seem to find it. This is an empty sac."

The first clear thought I remember having is that we had to start trying again: immediately. Like, go home, break out the KY, put a pillow over my face to soften the sobs and start trying again now, immediately. That's what I remember: the desperate urgency to make it the same again, to fill the empty.

My husband drove us to the hospital for confirmation lab work; I stared out the window, enraged. He tried to ask me if I was okay, and what I needed from him, and I half-tried to respond, but words caught in my throat like the oversized prenatal vitamins I'd been taking for over a month.

We didn't get to meet with the doctor for an explanation until the next day and by then, I'd already Googled my way to an amateur understanding of the empty sac. We'd had a blighted ovum, a chromosomal glitch in which the egg is fertilized but a fetus never starts to develop. It's a relatively common type of miscarriage. There never was a Fe. My body thought it was pregnant and apparently wouldn't figure out the growing sac was empty for a few more weeks. I found this to be very creepy. I also drank a bottle of wine, smoked several cigarettes, and chased it all with a final consciousness-erasing Ambien that night.

The doctor explained the pregnancy would naturally flush itself out within a few weeks, or they could give me a drug to expedite the process, or they could go in surgically and remove the sac. This procedure is called a D&C (short for dilation and curettage) to your face, and an MAB (or, missed abortion) behind your back. Either way, it's exactly what I wanted them to do. The practical joke had run its course. I was not pregnant with the start of a person, and I wasn't going to wait around for nature to run its course. Nature had her chance on this one, and I wasn't going to be screwed by her again. The scheduling coordinator told me the first opening she had for a D&C was a week away. I reached across the counter placing both my hands on hers, looked her right in the eyes, and said, "I can't go on carrying an empty sac around for a week. Please." She found an opening the following morning.

It was all for naught: the early hysteria, the relatively rapid acceptance, the C-cup breasts, the tiny onesies my mom sent me for Valentine's Day, the fourteen pounds, all of it. I'd read about developing heart chambers in week five, and tiny paddles where arms would be in week seven, and there was never anything there.

And quietly, irrationally, I wondered if I'd willed this whole thing out of existence, if my "Fetus, Fetus, go away" plea had worked. And if it had, I wanted a take-back. There were too many feelings to process in a month's time. First the now seemingly trivial fear that I'd lose myself with a baby in the picture (as though I've ever had a strong sense of identity rooted in anything greater than Vixen eyeliner), then there was the excitement, the authentic giddiness about the whole situation. A newborn by my birthday, a three-month old stocking stuffer to take home to the family at Christmas! And confusingly, bundled with the anger, emptiness and all together juvenile sense that "it's just not fair!" there was a tiny seed of excitement. I could diet away the evidence of conception. We could quit worrying about the economics of labor and delivery. Getting pregnant would be easy for me ... when the timing was exactly right. False alarm everybody, just go back to what you were doing . . . easy come, easy go.

I sent a well-crafted, nonchalant email to extended family, coworkers, and friends. We'd had a miscarriage, these things happen, we're fine, don't call us. I took slow deliberate drags of my Marlboros while assuring my husband I was not going to be one of those women who gets all dramatic and, "like, grieves the loss."

The day of the procedure I burst out laughing on the way to the doctor's office. My husband looked at me with both confusion and worry. I said, "Don't you think it's hilarious after all my indiscretions, that now-married and twenty-eight – my husband is driving me for an abortion?!" I think the irony was lost on him, but he didn't know me in college.

In as much as it was annoying and made me feel foolish, I think it was easier to think of an empty sac being sucked out of me than a kidney bean-sized person with distinctly webbed hands and feet. I don't remember much about the procedure, only that when we left the office, I couldn't shake the image of a gutted melon from my mind. I was back to work the next day.

I felt oddly numb. An adoring couple would push their couture stroller into the art gallery I manage and I'd look down at their perfect little baby cooing on cue and feel nothing. It was a strange and foreign sensation. "Your Pregnancy This Week" email updates continued to pop up in my inbox, and I met them with little more than a sarcastic huff and a click of the delete tab. I felt little desire to talk about it with anyone. I had no interest in journaling in part, because I didn't know what journal to write in. I didn't want to look at my pregnancy journal and my previous journal, which had "My FABULOUS Life" scrawled across the cover no longer seemed like an appropriate place to rest my thoughts.

Though my doctor told me to continue taking the prenatal vitamins, there was something desperate and sad about popping pills out of a package that had "it's about the baby" written across the box. No longer able to satisfy my appetite guilt-free, I threw away the remaining packages of pasta and a half carton of real vanilla ice cream. Finally, I slid the pregnancy magazines and books under my bed.

One of the most annoying things about miscarrying is that everyone you end up telling about the incident feels compelled to tell you their awesome miscarriage rebuttal story. They'll say, "My cousin Denise had three miscarriages in a row – bless her heart – and then she didn't get pregnant again for two years, but now, she has six kids." Or, "My friend Michelle had a miscarriage, and then she got pregnant with triplets three weeks later." If they don't happen to have a *Chicken Soup for the Miscarried Soul* story on hand, they'll say, "That always happens with the first pregnancy," or "It's Mother Nature's way," or "Everything happens for a reason." In total, I probably told three dozen people that I miscarried. Two of them looked me in the eye and said simply and sincerely, "I'm sorry."

I think the process of coming to terms with a miscarriage is muted for women who miraculously become pregnant in the early weeks and months after their loss. I thought this would be the case for me. My sister-in-law had a positive pregnancy test one day, a negative test and some bleeding three days later. And that was it – that was her miscarriage experience. She was pregnant less than a month later and delivered a healthy full-term baby boy the following December. That Christmas, the only thing my family fought over was who got to hold the newborn next and for how long.

I had two weeks after the D&C before "trying" was even an option. My husband encouraged me to take that time to decide what I wanted to do. From his perspective, he wasn't getting any younger. His mother died early of a heart attack, the same age her mother died of a heart attack. If we had a baby right now and my husband died at the same age as the two of them, little Junior would only be 24. It was a sobering thought, though I found it tender that he'd run the numbers in his head.

When I think back to those two weeks and my hysterical flip-flopping, I am amazed he never hit me over the head with a frying pan. I would retreat to my closet at night and hold a newborn onesie patterned with muted yellow ducks between my thumb and forefinger while staring in the mirror. Then I'd set it aside and hold up my Banana Republic skinny jeans, canting my head with similar affection and longing.

My chronic pelvic pain resumed soon after I got sex and exercise clearance from my doctor two weeks after the D&C. The unremitting ache was back, and short of another round of hormone therapy or surgery, there was really nothing western medicine could do for me. The prescription my doctor all but wrote out on a pad was simple: get pregnant. He said I could start trying again right away, though in a perfect world, he'd like me to wait one full cycle because it's easier to estimate a due date that way. I calculated, if it happened right away like it did for my sister-in-law, I could still have a baby by Christmas. Ultimately, I decided my desire for a baby coupled with my yearning to live without chronic pain outweighed my long time love affair with being a babe with a waist.

That's when it started: my husband's worst nightmare. I wanted to be pregnant and there was no un-ringing the bell. My resourceful online researching skills kicked in as I strove to better understand this business of baby-making.

I must have been staring out the window during health class throughout tenth grade, probably fantasizing about the non-sex, hot and heavy make out session I could have with my boyfriend once stupid seventh period was over. Had I paid attention, I would not have been nearly as shocked when I learned the woman kicks out an egg once a month, and if there's not already sperm in there loitering around from a previous encounter, there's only a 12-24 hour window to hurry up and have the sex again, because after that, that egg is dead and it's another month before you have another shot at it. I know this is simple human biology, but when you step back and look at all the things that have to line up exactly right to get a viable pregnancy going, you'll never look at a knocked-up teen cruising the aisles at Walmart the same way again.

When my first normal cycle resumed, I was relieved. It was my green light to start trying again. I read up on ovulation. The whole 14 day thing was a myth: the egg could burst through the ovary and make its way down the tube anytime between the 7th and the 20th day of cycle. Your body will give you clues as to when this is happening. You should keep the clues to yourself because no husband wants to hear, "I'm getting that egg white-like discharge, and that means ovulation is right around the corner. We should do it."

Always the extremist, I decided I could avoid awkward conversations about fertility by simply having sex every day during that "fertile window." Still, by the fourth consecutive day of my initiating forced and passionless copulation, my husband was on to me. I curled up to him and began tickling his arm with my fingernails, he rolled toward me and said gently, "Babe, why are you forcing this? Can you tell me why it's suddenly become so important and urgent?" It was a sincere ques-

tion, and I knew it deserved a sincere answer. With tears in my eyes I said, "Because I'm sick of being in pain." We both knew I was referring to the heavy, tearing, stabbing pain between my navel and the tops of my thighs, but as he started kissing me and his hands moved down my body, I realized I was talking about a different pain, one that had received much less attention than the endometriosis.

> . . . when you step back and look at all the things that have to line up exactly right to get a viable pregnancy going, you'll never look at a knocked-up teen cruising the aisles at Walmart the same way again.

The expected arrival date of my next period came and went. I took a home pregnancy test; it came up negative. Convinced I just wasn't a fast maker of the pregnancy hormone HCG detected in those tests, I walked around the house pressing my forearms against my breast saying, "Ouch. I must be pregnant. It really hurts when I apply great pressure to my chest." I bought ice cream and I ate it with abandon, as though stuffing my face would turn a pregnancy test pink. This was an exhausting little ritual for my science-minded husband. "If you're so sure you're pregnant, just take a test," he'd say. "I did that already, but it came back negative," I'd respond between spoonfuls of tortellini. Having retired early one night because, "the early pregnancy hormones were making me tired" (or perhaps because I'd worked three 10-hour days in a row), I sprang up from bed and sprinted to the living room. "Aha!" I announced, "You're making Top Ramen. I can smell it from the bedroom." I looked at him as though I'd just delivered the final clue in a murder mystery; he looked back at me wide-eyed and with maybe a little glimmer of fear. "Don't you see? Increased sense of smell?! Come on, it's so obvious." I skipped off to bed and fell asleep, Ambien-free thoughts of nursery themes and great names for triplets dancing in my head.

This monthly game is not uncommon among women who are TTC (fertility message board short-hand for: Trying To Conceive.) It was on those fertility message boards that I learned that feeling pregnant is not uncommon when you are trying desperately to get pregnant, especially when so many early pregnancy symptoms parallel PMS. These misinterpretations and delusions are commonly referred to as Imaginary Pregnancy Symptoms, though you won't find this term in the Physician's Desk Reference.

If you're wandering around the desert thirsty and depleted, you might experience an optical phenomenon that creates the illusion of water, you might see a mirage. For me, the months after the miscarriage felt like months spent in open and lonely desert terrain. I didn't feel justified mourning the miscarriage, and so I put all my energy and emotion into getting pregnant again. It seemed to me miscarriages are sad because you lose a pregnancy, and if I could just get pregnant again, the sadness I couldn't quite pinpoint or acknowledge might at last abate.

I no longer feel numb when I see a darling little pregnant lady standing in line at the supermarket . . .

I sat in my therapist's office a few months after the whole ordeal, neither pregnant nor pre-pregnant thin. I explained that I wasn't sad, but I did feel pissed. The whole stupid fire drill had been a hoax; I felt like I'd been punk'd. Now, something that hadn't even popped into my mind in a serious way was all I could think about. When I wasn't thinking about getting pregnant again, I was thinking about everything I'd done wrong in the last one. I felt like there was no one in my life that could understand the complexity of these feelings, how I could go from wishing away an embryo to feeling such anger at its non-existence in a matter of weeks. Fe may have always been a figment of my uterus' imagination, but she'd become very real to me.

I told her I was having trouble seeing, that the borders of everything from trees to text messages looked blurry to me, and I didn't know why. Nothing tasted much like anything, and all that I felt like doing when I wasn't faking "fine" at work was drinking wine and watching reality TV. I told her something was terribly wrong with my stomach and bowels and that no amount of Pepto or Imodium made it feel right. She let me verbally vomit on her for several more minutes, and when at last I stopped for air she said, "What you're describing is grief."

There was a long, dare I say, pregnant pause. We stared at each other pupil to pupil and then, for the first time since the empty sac ultrasound day, I lost it. I cried from that place in my stomach that was never soothed by pink syrup and between sobs I didn't bother to judge myself or the implausibility of sadness in this situation. Still obviously heavily invested in the anger / bargaining stage of grief, I blurted, "I don't want to feel this. I want to go back to the way I felt before this all happened, or I want to be pregnant again. I don't want to live in this space between. It's too uncomfortable." She nodded that nod they teach therapists on the first day of graduate school, and then she said, "I know it's uncomfortable, but it's where you are right now, and it's where your work is right now."

My work right now: this sticky, ill-fitting, lonely space between is where I am supposed to be working. I can't re-do the

first 9 weeks of my first pregnancy, and I can't will conception to happen any faster than it's apparently going to happen. We have conceived before, we will likely be able to conceive again. In the meantime, I am trying not to reduce my life to monthly cycles divided by follicular and luteal phases. I have been late each month since the D&C. Some months I go 38 days between periods, others, it's more like 50. My female intuition tells me this irregularity is caused at least in part by stress.

I no longer feel numb when I see a darling little pregnant lady standing in line at the supermarket, and when I overhear her tell the checker she is due in September, I acknowledge the pang of longing and the sense of injustice it makes me feel inside and often, as my therapist suggested, I say in my head, *hello, sadness.*

Recently we were watching a movie on a Friday night. In the final scene a woman took a home pregnancy test in the bathroom, it came up positive and she ran out of the house chasing her husband down the street with the stick in her hand. Before the thought could seek pre-approval in my frontal lobe I heard myself say aloud, "Don't get too excited. It could just be an empty sac." My husband looked at me with both surprise and sympathy, and I said to myself, *hello, anger.*

Like all women TTC, I get anxious every month as day 29 and 30 of my cycle pass. I still press my arms against my chest and wonder if it's more sensitive than normal; then I wonder if that sensitivity is PMS or pregnancy. But I no longer drive to the doctor's office demanding a blood test because I'm convinced home pregnancy tests just aren't sensitive enough to detect levels of HCG in me. This, I think, is progress. When I start to bleed a few days later, I usually indulge in a few hours of cognitive acrobatics. *What if I can't get pregnant again? What if that was our one shot? What's wrong with me? Why is it taking so long? Should I go buy an ovulation kit to make sure that's happening or would that just make me more stressed and make this harder? What if whatif what if . . . Hello, anxiety.* Sometimes I find myself imagining my feelings as a baby pressed against my chest. I pat them on the back as though I'm soothing my newborn while whispering, *I know. I know.*

Fe was like that guy whose advances are met with disdain, a guy who gloms onto you and annoys you until one day he makes a joke that leaves you in stitches or notices something about you that you never thought anyone would get. From there, you warm up to him. You start enjoying his company and moreover, you enjoy your own company more when you're with him because you are a better, more self-actualized version of yourself when he's around. And that warm calmness you feel when you're together is a feeling you slowly start to recognize as love. And then, as quickly and in as strange of way as he came in to your life, he is gone. And you are left once again with yourself, scratching your head and wondering how another good one got away. You must resume the work of trying to enjoy your own company without your built-in buddy. This is the work that waits for you in the space between the one that got away and the next great love that awaits you.

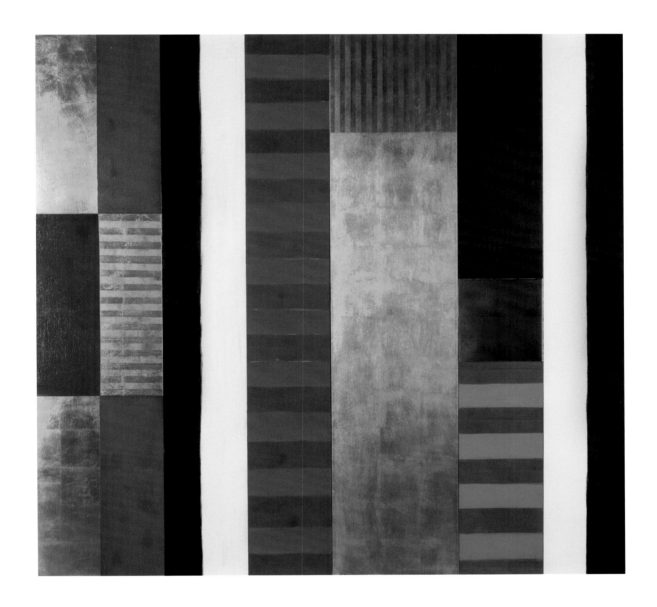

Byzantium (Black Sea)

Steve Joy
media media on panel

Threshold

Graceann Warn
oil and encaustic on canvas

Greg Kosmicki

The Night I Hear Beef Torrey is Dying

I'm on the computer with a technician
from the Philippines named Ruby
who laughs and said she doesn't
want to be called Ruby Ann even though
that's the name that pops up on the screen
when she comes on to take over
my computer to fix it, and I've been
on the phone with Ruby and some guy
from India for the last hour when Debbie
walks in with a note that says
Beef Torrey's organs are all shut down
but I can't get off the computer
they're heading up to the hospital
because I've been on it now for hours
he's going to go into hospice
and they've got to wipe out my hard drive
there's no chance of an organ transplant.
So the night I pick to finally call Hewlett Packard
a guy I've known for 30 years or more
gets so sick he's going to die
and I can't hang up the phone.
OK if it were one of my own kids or my wife
I would but I know Beef
would say not to worry man
so I finish up the computer call
come down from the office and try his friend's numbers
and pour myself a whiskey.
Then I drink it, and write this out for Beef.

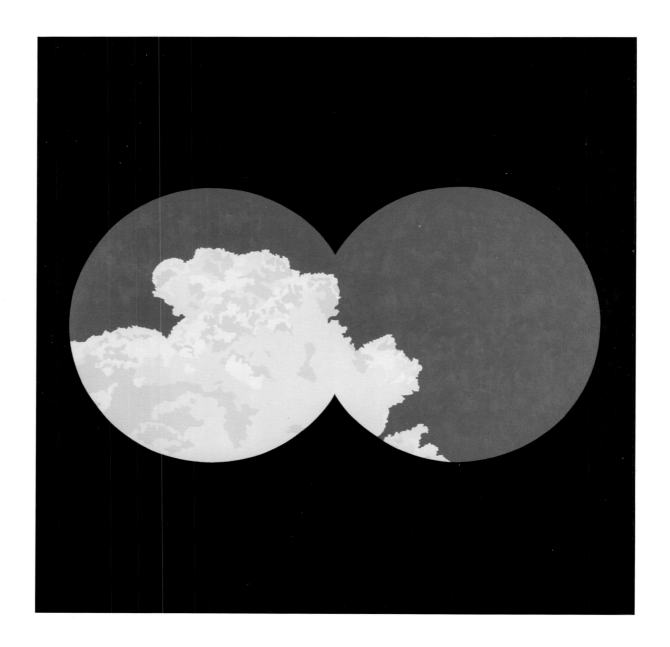

Binoculared Clouds

Benjamin Pratt
acrylic on canvas

Linda Bagshaw

Epiphany

All I ever knew
of the ocean
were flat blue spaces
spread across my
schoolbook maps
and curved around
the glossy globe
that I would trace
with curious fingers.
And all I ever knew was
what I read of
salt and seaweed,
sandy edges, rising tides,
rushing waves and
scattered shells.
Then one bright
and pristine day,
my dad drove further
than I'd ever been,
far east to where
that ocean was
said to be.
And before I ever saw
the shining blue
or stubbed my toe
on hidden shells,
I caught the salty scent
of ocean breath
and knew it
all was true.

Twyla M. Hansen

Sorting

Picture him amid the rust – hand tools, jars of screws,
bolts, half-useful wrenches – assembling miniature farm
wagons, windmills, trains, as if one day he would return.

And return he does – in the various and sundry nails,
boxes of brads, wood scraps, lengths of wire thick
with dust – as the *waste not want not* farmer.

Which fills you with regret: not spending more time,
not listening, not facing what you could not save.

Now, you empty the pegboard of worn coping saw blades,
the calendar with pig photos and corny quotes,
toss handles, staples, hinges, caulk, tape, string, metal, and

weep, knowing this is as close as you will ever be to him,
his world reduced to tinkering alone down in this city cave,
touching what his rough hands touched, his curiosities,

your father under a bare bulb sawing pieces of his last
unfinished project, a sea-faring ship, its instructions and
pattern carefully numbered and folded – the glued, carved

and sanded balsawood – as if he sensed this full-blown
final creation might help him sail across that ancient sea.

Shards 2

John Beckelman
fired ceramics, concrete, and mixed media

Pat Underwood

The Return

Thousands of us celebrate
the Fourth of July, sitting in grasses
surrounded by lilies and Iowa Rose.
Simon Estes sings *Old Man River,*
and the stage releases a flock of doves.
Our necks bend to catch the white flutter
of peace against an overcast sky.

When twilight melts to evening,
I wait for him to call – a trust
as in the fountain near me
with its return and replenish,
return and replenish, tier after tier
of soothing flow. He texts. After
our long wait we exchange messages,
a touch of fingertips, a door opening,
a shift of air.

I tell you, that which you fear,
that which you take to be over –
abruptly ended – can be a sweet return
to a more gentle place.
Like the doves' coming back
before flying off to a new home.

Jesse Breite

Fields of Light

When I see the Mississippi River Basin
and its meanders mapped
flat, dry and sprawling at home
in Atlanta, I can feel its pulse –
silver ripple out of blue.
It's arterial still, and exacting
as copper through ivy.

With the back of my hand,
I can almost dip into the water
and bring it to my lips. I know
the velvet touch of maculate wounds,
the warm presence of nerve-bundles.

My father is driving I-55 over the river
in Memphis. His big black truck
trembles on the iron spine.
On the other side, the land is flush.
Shadows glide over bean
and rice fields ahead of him.

His dry knuckles crack and bleed
on the cold steering wheel.
Oblong stones burn into the earth
the way absence burns.
The atmosphere is full of so much
that hasn't happened.

We are nothing if not still, closer now
than before. Light can rip
and flower from shapeless blankets
of space as if every speck
was made to shimmer in brevities,
as if unknown communions
could hold every shard together.

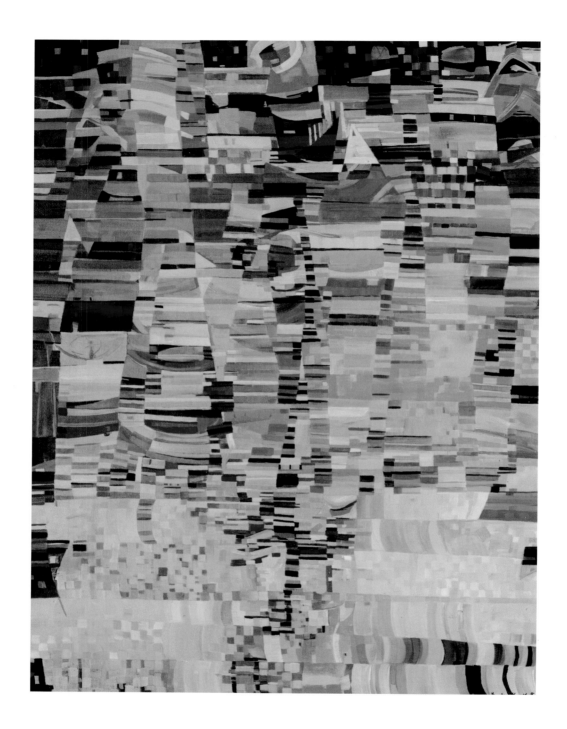

In Due Time

Jacqueline Kluver
acrylic on canvas

Barbara Duffey

Inclined Plane

I'm a non-scientist –
I shoot this obliquely:

If you screw and screw with
still no body housed in

your overfolded frame,
you will be subject to

platitudinism:
it's not in God's plan, it

wasn't meant to be, you
wouldn't be given more

than you could jinny down
that radical needle

of motion, kinetic
thrust of time, perhaps your

house twists with truncated
genes. Yet I felt my child

like a compass needle
in night navigation

slanting, right as polar
pull, some slip-way in my

tilt, his runabout nerves.
I semi-shelved him till

the doctor and his art,
that acceleration

of my milk and family,
somehow returned me to

subsistent skin. In a
word, he was weight, he was

strong, pitched, wedged in there, mine
and striking with small soles.

David Watts

Pause

All day I'm in shelter
on a granary floor, rain
on the roof like buckshot
in branches. Aroma
of wet earth, dry
grain. The air unhurried
and intentional. I have made
a chair of hay bales, spread
a saddle blanket. Contained
womb-like against the heft
of the out-of-doors, there is
this soft heartbeat of contentment.
The dark print of my life
outside the walls.
It knows the rain will stop.

Lucia Cherciu

Horse Chestnuts in Bloom

When we got home
I wrapped myself in his overcoat,
his *şubă*, and curled up in bed
like a fetus and tried to sleep.

The coat smelled like him.
He kept it for clean,
didn't wear it on his job
on the milk truck with ungodly hours
from two A.M. till noon
delivering milk to all the stores in town
lifting the crates on and off the ramp.

I left the lights on
the way somebody said
we were supposed to do for forty days.

Outside it was already warm.
The first week in May
the horse chestnuts were blooming,
their candelabra reaching
close to the balcony
on the fifth floor,
flowers splurging
too late or too soon.

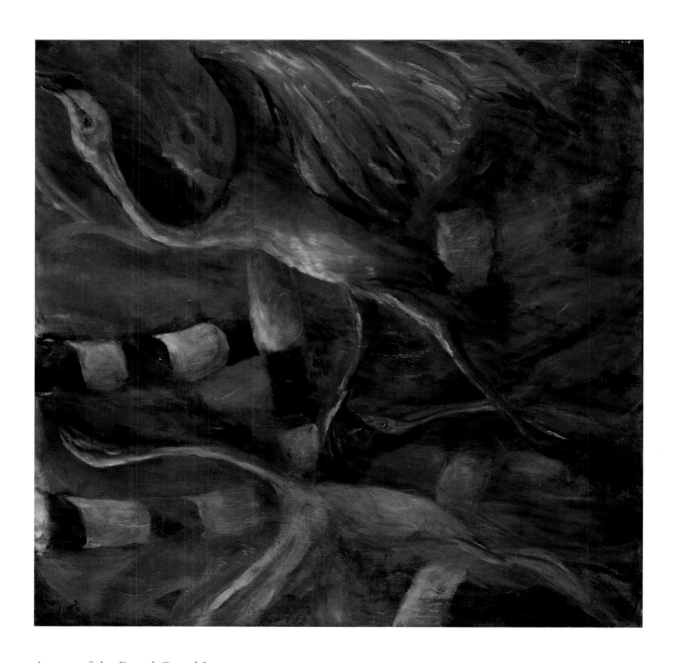

Ascent of the Royal Guard I

Ann Marie McTaggart
oil and mixed media on canvas

Rachel Ann Girty

Sammā-diṭṭhi

Night: each building the same
Oil-red catch of cold in the scrolled
Texturelessness of afterglow.

Smoke shifts along the absent
Horizon, breath in the emptiness
Between taste and memory of taste.

You live miles from here, the sliding
Of streets is a strange arrangement here,
The descant of wind a wider recursion

Here through the backseat window
Where the smell of the old world
Is blunted by cigarette butts

And exhaust and menstruation.
You disintegrate into the night
Faster than the night into you,

Residue collecting residue – sound
And color spilling into this taxi
And soon you'll abandon it all for home.

Somewhere in the distance a flame
Goes out: tonight is in the past
Already – you can feel it forgetting itself,

Pistons pounding each atom of the city
Away, but every gasp of air before you
Waits a threshhold. A city of reds

Blooming night's distances to heat.
When the engine stops, you aren't home.
You've never seen this blossom of firebrick

Before but you know how it grows
Around you at dawn – you know where
Its shadows are, its passageways.

Outside time is hotter than you imagined
And it takes your edges with it as it burns.
Learn to walk through the fire.

Personal Wealth

Louise Marburg

Julian's wife Laura had been depressed for over five months, and was still unwell when they visited Todd and Rose on the cape in August, though when Julian thought about it, paged back through their marriage, he realized she had been gradually sinking for years. But it had been five months since she'd been hospitalized for attempting to take her own life by slicing her wrists with a paring knife, fortunately botching the job. There had been plenty of blood, but not a fatal amount. She was still conscious when Julian found her sitting on the edge of the tub, blood dripping from her wrists into a spreading pond on the tiles. People, their friends and families, asked him if he'd had "any idea," a question so stupid he could hardly bring himself to reply. Obviously if he had known the depth of Laura's despair he would have gotten her the appropriate help. *Why hadn't he known the depth of her despair?* That was the unspoken question. "But I told you," Laura said when he asked her why she'd done it, "I told you I want to die." Had she? Yes, she had. She'd said exactly that. But people said all sorts of dramatic things they didn't mean. He hadn't paid any attention. The surface of their lives remained calm. Then the reckoning: the blood and the ambulance and the hospital, the doctors and the drugs. He was paying attention now.

She stood at the water's edge, Rose by her side. Rose and Todd's son, Zach, held Rose by the hand. He pranced around on the glistening sand, his voice piping over the growl of the waves: "Mommy please, Mommy no, why Mommy, why not." Julian could tell by the set of Laura's shoulders that Zach was bothering her. He was the kind of child who believed that everything and everyone was available to him (he'd taken Julian's glass of lemonade right out of his hand at lunch) and that his presence was always appreciated, but Laura was sensitive to noise and chaos; the latest antidepressant she was trying out made her dizzy if she moved her head too quickly. It also made her put on weight. She and Rose used to have similar figures, tall and slim and small-breasted, but now Laura's body looked almost square in her tank suit: the extra weight had settled between her shoulders and hips, making her legs look like frail supports. She strode into the water and dove under a foaming, green wave. Julian waited until her head popped up before looking down at his magazine. Todd sat in a canvas beach chair, reading a paperback. He and Julian were not as close as the women, who had known each other since college, but they were friends, Julian thought. Yet Todd hadn't said much to either him or Laura since they arrived the evening before.

Julian closed his magazine. He had been reading about ISIS and didn't care to know more. The scent of the sunblock he had rubbed on his arms and chest reminded him of every summer of his life. "Hey Todd, everything good with you these days? How's the law business going?"

"Fantastic," Todd said. "You? Still killing it in Personal Wealth?"

"Killing it," Julian said automatically. He worked for a bank in its Personal Wealth department, making sure clients were satisfied with their investment portfolios. It was a pleasant job, not terribly demanding; his salary was a sliver of Todd's. In the good old days, as Julian thought of them, Todd and Rose and he and Laura used to rent houses together in various areas on the cape for a couple of weeks every summer. The houses inevitably had more bedrooms than they needed, so they invited friends to visit; something interesting was always happening, or about to happen, or being talked about. But a few years ago, after Zach was born, Todd bought one of the houses, a shingled contemporary in Wellfleet that overlooked the beach. It was Julian's favorite of the handful they had rented, and he'd been shocked and frankly resentful when Laura told him the news. Now they visited Todd and Rose in the house the four of them had shared. Julian and Laura were demoted from co-hosts to guests, and instead of two weeks, they came for a few days.

Todd went back to reading his book. Julian watched Laura swim. It was a blue and white day, and the sea was choppy; a strand of fair-weather clouds hovered over the horizon. Rose held Zach on her hip and waded into the water. He could see the women were talking, and wondered what about. After a while, Laura waded out, and Rose stayed in with Zach.

"Hey baby," he said as she approached, combing her wet hair with her fingers. She'd chopped it chin-short a year ago and hadn't let it grow out. She was a lovely-looking woman, dark-haired and brown-eyed with pale, unblemished skin, and dimples in her cheeks when she smiled. Snow White, he called her when they were dating and first married. She smiled at him, but her eyes were tired. Exhaustion was another side effect of the medication she was taking. "How're you feeling?" he asked as he stood and wrapped a dry towel around her shoulders.

"Okay," she said. "I'm going up to the house."

"Do you want me to come with you?"

"Of course not!" she said in a laughing voice he knew was meant for Todd. She was ashamed of being depressed ("mentally ill," or just "mental," was how she described herself when she was feeling wry) and gotten so good at acting cheerful that sometimes even Julian was fooled. He watched her trudge off through the sand, and climb the silvery wooden steps to the house, slower now than she was before – again, an effect of the medicine. The three antidepressants she'd tried so far had failed to lift her mood, but all of them made her feel physically ill. He had to stop himself from going after her as he watched her disappear into the house. "Killing yourself is harder to accomplish than you'd think," the psychiatrist at the hospital had told him. "Only one in thirty people who try it succeed, and those who don't are usually glad they didn't." Laura hadn't said she was glad to be alive, but she understood it wasn't just herself she would hurt if she tried suicide again. He knew that she would scold him for following her. He sat down again in his beach chair. The house was in his line of sight.

> The wrinkle that appeared above the bridge of her nose told him she was onto his thoughts.

Rose came out of the water with Zach and set him on a towel with a bag of sand castle molds. What ever happened to using your imagination? Julian remembered the complicated fortresses he'd constructed as a child and the moats he dug around them, running back and forth from the water's edge with dripping handfuls of sand. Zach made a lopsided tower with a mold, then savagely knocked it down.

"Don't kick sand onto the grownups, Zachie," Rose said as she sat down in the chair next to Julian. She let out a breath and said, "Isn't this nice?"

"Beautiful day," he said. "Thanks so much for having us."

"Of course!" she said with too much emphasis, which made Julian think that she and Todd had considered *not* inviting them this year. Which one of them had demurred, and which had prevailed? Or had both of them had their doubts? A

startling amount of friends had gone to ground in the wake of Laura's episode. At first Laura had been too dazed to notice, then she was dismayed, then hurt. Julian made her see she was better off without them, saying, "Now you know who your real friends are." Rose had been one of the first people to visit Laura after she was released from the hospital, though caring for Zach made it difficult for her to get out: she and Laura talked on the phone. But Zach was three now, Julian realized, old enough for school. He watched the boy fill a mold with sand.

"Where does Zach go to school?" he asked.

"St. Mary's," Rose said.

"What do you do when he's there?"

"Well, it's preschool, he's only there half a day. I go to the gym, grocery shop, you know, stuff like that."

"Meet friends for coffee?"

"Oh, sure."

Julian looked down the beach as if there was something interesting to see: walkers, picnickers, children dancing in the surf. Having put her PhD in Linguistics on hold until an effective medication was found, Laura was often at loose ends during the day. Going out for coffee with Rose now and then would have raised her spirits, but obviously that was an effort Rose didn't care to make.

"You get together with other moms, I imagine. Talk about mom stuff."

The wrinkle that appeared above the bridge of her nose told him she was onto his thoughts. "Zachie, here, let me show you," she said. She filled a mold. "Very carefully, turn it over. See? Perfect."

"I don't like it," Zach said.

She sighed and smiled at Julian. "Thinking of having one of these rascals any time soon? It's a lot more fun than it looks."

Julian didn't know how to respond. Laura would never "recover;" she would have to take medication for the rest of her life. Her psychiatrist wanted to try a mood stabilizer now, and if that didn't work, an antipsychotic. "You don't have to be psychotic to take an antipsychotic," he assured Laura, as if she cared. "I'll take anything," she'd told Julian. "I'll do anything. I'd have a lobotomy if it would make me feel like living." They had planned on having children after she finished her PhD. He didn't care if she never finished; children were unimportant. Her happiness was the only thing he wanted, her continued existence in his life.

The expression on his face made Rose stop smiling. "Sorry. Sometimes I forget."

"Well, don't," he said.

She drew back. "You don't have to be harsh, Julian. She doesn't seem as depressed as she did right after...you know. Honestly, she seems pretty okay to me."

"She puts on good show," Julian said. "But don't believe it, she feels like hell."

Rose nodded and said, "I guess everyone has a cross to bear. I'm sorry Laura's is so heavy." She glanced at Todd, who was still engrossed in his book. *So her cross was her husband,*

Julian thought with surprise. He'd always considered Rose and Todd to be a perfectly matched couple – more so, in fact, than he and Laura, who was far and away better educated. But he took nothing for granted anymore; people's lives were just as likely as not to be the opposite of how they appeared.

"What?" she said. "Why are you looking at me?"

"No reason. I think I'll get a beer. Want anything?"

Rose shook her head.

He felt released as he ran up the steps to the house. The room where they were staying had a view of the beach; it was the same one they'd stayed in when they rented the place. He opened the door a crack. A breeze whistled though the half-open windows, twisting the sheer curtains into streamers. He didn't dare step in for fear of making a sound. Curled up like an infant, her face crushed into a pillow, Laura was asleep on the bed.

In the early evening, another couple arrived whom Julian and Laura didn't know. Rose and Todd greeted them – Barbara and Geoff – as if they were long-lost friends. *So* glad to see them, *what* a treat, *such* luck that they could come. Barbara was an attorney; Geoff had his own architectural firm. Before having Zach, Rose had been an interior designer, so when she showed Geoff the house, which he immediately asked to see, she used professional terms to describe basic things like windows and baseboards and floors. Geoff was older and had a bald, spotty head with a gray fringe grazing the back of his collar. Barbara was thirty-ish and attractive in a bony-faced way that would serve her well as she got older. Julian and Laura had brought so few clothes that they had been able to pack them all in a single small bag, so when Barbara and Geoff wheeled in a pair of matching carry-ons, Laura frowned at Julian and went to their room. That Barbara and Geoff had been asked to stay longer than Julian and Laura was Julian's first thought, but Laura was doubtless worrying that she hadn't brought the right things to wear. Rose hadn't said anything about the other couple until a minute before they arrived.

"I knew you wouldn't come if I told you," she said while Todd showed Barbara and Geoff to their room. She wore a pair of white slacks and a colorful top, suddenly all dressed up.

"You're right, we wouldn't have," Julian said in a low voice. They were in the living room, the most central area of the house, and its ceiling was an echoing pyramid. "Socializing with strangers is hard on Laura."

"I'm sorry," Rose said. "Todd invited them. He didn't run it by me. Apparently this was the only weekend they were available. Truthfully? I would have preferred a weekend alone with you and Laura. But Todd asked me to entertain them, and I really felt I had to."

"Why?" Julian said. "What's so special about them?"

She shrugged. "Barbara is interviewing for a position in Todd's firm. He says he needs to get to know her socially to see if she's a good fit. Just be nice to them, okay? Laura can slip out whenever she wants."

Wearing a simple sundress, Laura reappeared just as Todd escorted Geoff and Barbara back to the living room. Like Rose, Barbara was wearing white slacks and sandals, but her top was a dramatically flowing caftan embellished with embroidery and sequins. In Julian's opinion, Laura looked beautiful, and the other two looked tarted up, but he felt Laura's self-consciousness like a current: *I'm hideous*, he could hear her thinking. Though she wasn't meant to drink alcohol in combination with her medication, she accepted a glass of wine from Rose, and visibly relaxed as she drank it. They all went out to the deck to watch the sun's gaudy descent while Todd barbequed a slab of beef. Zach ran around with a seagull's feather twined in his hair, flapping his arms, and screeching. Rose bribed him away with a video, and the promise of ice cream later.

"That's quite a hunk of meat," Barbara said as she joined Todd by the grill.

"Are you a lawyer too?" Geoff asked Julian. The way he held his wine glass against his chest made Julian think he was gay.

"No, I'm in Personal Wealth."

"Ah," Geoff said, and moved on to Laura. "And you?"

"Me? I'm a…" She shook her head and started again. "I'm getting my PhD in Linguistics."

"Laura and I were roommates our junior and senior years!" Rose said brightly. "She was *such* a smarty-pants."

"A PhD! I'm impressed. I could hardly get through three years of architecture school."

"I almost didn't graduate from college," Rose said with a laugh.

Laura raised her eyebrows. Julian followed her gaze. She was looking at Todd and Barbara, who stood chatting by the grill. They clinked glasses and smiled at each other. So Barbara was a good fit. Laura looked at Julian. *What?* he mouthed. *Later*, she mouthed back. Rose went into the kitchen to slice some tomatoes, and Geoff asked if he could help.

"Aren't we popular," Julian said. "Cleared the room. Now tell me. What?"

She scooted closer to him on the bench they shared. "Todd and Barbara are fucking," she said. Her voice and manner were so like the old Laura that Julian was startled.

He smiled because she was smiling. "Why do you say that?"

"Because I saw Todd squeeze Barbara's ass."

"No. Really? When?"

"Just now! And Barbara did not object." She picked up the wine bottle, and poured herself a second glass. Julian decided not to say anything about it; he couldn't remember the last time he'd seen her so lighthearted, and a couple of glasses wouldn't make any difference. He looked at Barbara's full breasts and wide hips – such a different type than lithe Rose – and wondered which one of them, she or Todd, had initiated the affair. She poked Todd's chest with her forefinger, and he laughed for what seemed to Julian like the first time since he and Laura arrived.

That afternoon, while Laura was napping, and Rose was playing in the waves with Zach, Todd had asked for the first time how Laura was doing.

"Not great, to be honest," Julian said. "It's been a longer haul than we anticipated."

Todd stretched out his arms and yawned. His biceps bulged, his thighs were sinewy and thick. Julian could count the muscles in his stomach. "Not exactly what you signed up for, huh."

"What isn't?" Julian said.

"Having your wife go bonkers."

Julian stared at him. "She's not 'bonkers,' she's depressed, and yes, I did in fact sign up for it. In sickness and in health? Ever heard of it?"

Todd shook his head. "No offense, buddy. I admire your loyalty, hanging in there and all that, but if Rose pulled that shit I'd be out of here, pronto."

"Laura didn't *pull* anything, Todd. I hang in there because I love her."

> Her expression was stony, her lips pressed tight. Tipsy had flipped to belligerent in a blink.

"Good for you," he said and picked up his paperback again. Julian felt dismissed and no less insulted; Todd might as well have called him a sucker.

Rose brought a platter of tomatoes to the table, and Geoff followed with a basket of corn on the cob. Barbara and Todd were the last to sit down. Julian felt Laura's bare foot touch his shin and was pleasantly turned on.

"What were you two talking about over there?" Laura said to Barbara.

"Oh, just business," Barbara said.

"Really? Because it looked like you were having a lot of fun. I almost joined you, but then I thought I might be intruding." She gave them a dimply grin.

"Not at all!" Barbara said. Julian saw she didn't know about Laura. "Todd is in the middle of a difficult case, a merger between two private companies." She leaned forward to include everyone in the conversation. Todd ate his steak as if none of them existed. "The CEOs are both about a thousand years old and utterly set in their ways. Todd says they're like spoiled children, he has to handle them with kid gloves." She shook her frosty hair down her back and looked across the table at Rose. "I'm sure you've heard about it chapter and verse, Rose. Your husband is heroic."

Rose opened her mouth and closed it like a goldfish sucking air. She gathered herself and said, "Oh, sure, chapter and verse. Todd tells me everything that goes on in his life."

Todd looked up from his plate. "If I told you everything that goes on in my life you'd probably divorce me tomorrow." If he was trying to be funny, no one could tell; they were silent until Geoff asked if anyone wanted more wine. When Laura

pushed her glass forward, Julian almost pulled it back, but he didn't want to embarrass her.

"Julian!" Geoff said in a fake, hearty voice. "Tell us about Personal Wealth."

"There's not a lot to tell. Basically my job is to take care of the bank's major clients, make sure that they're happy. I take them to lunch, I advise them on how much they can spend; I make sense of their statements for them if they can't understand them themselves, and explain the hows and whys of their investments. An awful lot of very rich people are ignorant about their money."

"A lot of people are ignorant, period," Laura said. Her expression was stony, her lips pressed tight. Tipsy had flipped to belligerent in a blink. Julian tried to catch her eye, but she was looking angrily at her plate. The glass of wine that Geoff had just poured her was already three-quarters gone.

Geoff chuckled. "So says the PhD."

"I'm not a PhD," she said. "I'm mentally ill." Barbara and Geoff laughed at that. Rose reached across the table and touched her hand. Laura looked at Geoff. "No, I'm serious. I tried to kill myself. Rose didn't tell you?"

"Of course I didn't," Rose said softly.

"Oh, for God's sake, Laura, give it a rest," Todd said. "So you're unhappy, you're *depressed*. Isn't everybody, more or less?" His face was florid from standing over the hot grill. He raised his fork like a scepter. "Happiness is something you have to *go* for. You've got to grab the brass ring when you can."

Laura studied the green-gold wine in her glass, turning it by its stem. "Grab some ass, you mean."

"Laura!" Rose said at the same moment as Todd said, "So what if I do?"

"I want ice cream!" Zach appeared, wearing nothing but his underpants.

Julian took Laura back to their room, helped her undress, and watched her fall asleep before undressing himself and lying down next to her. Who knew what would have happened if Zach hadn't shown up. He could have punched Todd – he wished he had – or maybe Rose would have yanked Barbara's over-dyed hair. Geoff might have suddenly announced he was gay. Dramas worthy of a reality show floated through his mind. That he and Laura were being talked about now was an absolute certainty, excuses made, apologies offered, walls of denial being built. How convenient that Laura was ill: it accounted for so much. He turned and very gently took her hand, turned it palm up, and ran his thumb over the raised scar on her wrist. "You don't love me," she'd said in the hospital, not as an accusation but a fact, her voice so quiet and accepting that he knew she'd thought so for a long time. Had she been awake now she wouldn't have let him look at her scars, but he considered them indelible reminders, important to see, that he nearly lost the most valuable person on earth. The inessential had fallen away from his life as the scales had fallen from Saul's eyes. Laura sighed and turned over. Reluctantly, he released her hand.

He felt as if he'd only slept for a minute, but the clock on his phone read past midnight. It had still been light outside when he fell asleep; now he was wide awake. He reached for Laura, but felt only a rumpled sheet.

In a single movement, he was on his feet. Smelling of toothpaste and Geoff's aftershave, the guest bathroom was dark and empty. There was a small lamp in the living room that someone had forgotten to turn off, and for a moment he thought he saw Laura sitting in its warm circle of light. The kitchen was dim and tidy; the refrigerator sighed. Barefoot, he ran out to the deck. He could hear his own breathing as he stumbled down the steps, splinters snagging his flesh. The tide was high and the ocean glassy, reflecting a moon that lit the whole beach. Even so, he almost fell over her. She sat with her knees pulled up to her chin, looking out at the water.

"Jesus," he said as he dropped into the cold sand. He put his palm to his chest and felt his heart booming. "What are you doing, Laura? Why are you out here?"

"I'm sorry, I'm sorry!" She pulled him to her and cradled his head against her neck. He could feel her pulse pumping in concert with his heart. "I wasn't thinking about you, I'm such an idiot!" She let him go. "I am so selfish. It didn't even occur to me that you might wake up."

Julian took a long breath and touched his head to his knees. He sat up and said, "You're okay."

"I am." Her face was pale in the moonlight, her eyes lightless, black. "I really made a mess tonight, didn't I. Rose probably hates me now."

He didn't answer. It seemed that Laura and Rose's relationship would change at the very least. He put his arm around her. Her sweater felt warm against his bare arm.

"You know, every night I pray to God, or whoever is out there and might be listening to me." She stared at the sea as she spoke. "I pray every night that when I wake up the next morning I will see the sun in our window and be glad it's a new day. And every morning I wake up and the day is gray, and I want to die, and nothing has changed." She looked at him. "I do that. I pray. I close my eyes and clasp my hands, like a kid asking God for a pony or some other impossible thing. Isn't that stupid?"

"No," Julian said. He hadn't known she did this. The desperation of it brought tears to his eyes: neither of them believed in God, or any deity.

She put her fist to her forehead. "It hurts, you know. Physically."

He nodded. She had said this before. "What else does it feel like?" he asked, though she'd told him many times.

"It's like seeing the world through a veil, everything is the same color. When I imagine the future I see nothing, a blank wall. If someone asks me a simple question, I feel like I can hardly find the words to answer. My mind is empty. I crawl from minute to minute until the day is over. And then I pray, and go to sleep. And then I wake up unchanged." She was silent then. The waves crashed in and gurgled out; a cricket chirped from the dunes. The windows of the houses along the beach were black, though a few porch lights sliced the dark. "What's going to happen to me?" she finally said.

> "And every morning I wake up and the day is gray, and I want to die, and nothing has changed."

"You're going to get better," he said, as he always did. It was a song they sang together.

"When?"

"I don't know when, but I know you will."

"You sound so sure."

"Because I am."

"How do you know?"

"I just do."

"I wouldn't ask for anything else in life, that would be enough."

"Oh, but you'll have so much more."

She leaned into him. He smelled the sea in her hair, the mothballs from her sweater. "I wish the sun would come up so we can go home. What time is it now? Can we wait here?"

Julian shivered. It would be hours until dawn. "Of course we can wait," he said.

Chuck

Michael Frizzell
oil on canvas

Barbara Saunier

Losing the Count, Regaining the World

In the house now burn fewer lights – one
near the window where nights she sits
with her knitting, soothing
as lanolin. She can't even guess – socks?
A cap. Or scarf? A tea cozy?
The knitted folds that shawl her lap
spill either side of her knees, a pool
of loops intersecting loops. Stitches –
Who's counting?

In a fairy tale, she might tell unfinished stories
for a thousand and one nights, might
grow her hair long as a tower
is tall. (A receiving blanket?
An afghan for the day bed maybe.) She would ride
on the backs of beavers needling upstream
to knit themselves a hearth from whatever's
at hand. She would become the beaver.

Her shrewd hands assume the wit
to stem a breach at the sound of water
seeping. Over long weeks,
her light burns, and waves of knitted folds
pond the floor. The day she finally looks up,
it's not a cap or sweater spread before her,
but a lodge cozy. An acreage. A wide, still water.

– With thanks to KW

Invisible

Sadie Martin
photograph

Mineral

Corey Broman
blown, sand-carved, wheel-cut glass, steel, and wood

Patricia Fargnoli

My Father Whose Death

My father whose death impels me to speak,
whose eyes were storm clouds
and whose hair was black water,
my father who stood far above me
in his gray wool coat and fedora.

My father whose face was anguish,
who loved opera and alcohol,
who sold magazines and Christmas trees,
my father whom I worshiped,
his arm around my ten-year-old shoulders.

My father the unforeseen who chose to leave
my father the dark shabby hotel room
my father the chair the rope the noose
who leapt from failure to failure.

My father you were not illumination, not
three yellow kittens, not a tiger god,
not a migration of geese,
nor a companion for the journey.
You went your own way
and did not consider me.

But you were also a fairytale, a chariot,
whose eyes were black walnuts, whose hair
shone with silver. My father weren't you also
a carousel ride, a question mark?
When I remember you, a window opens
into the old house of my dreams
where you appear holding ashes.

O ancient father who keeps returning,
will I ever be done with you?
And yet I loved, love, am loving you.
Sometimes it is as if I am still
talking to you in spite of the leaving,
chattering along as though you were hiding here
under dead leaves in the desolate garden.

Garden Arbor

Michael Walsh
photograph

Dandarians, Lee Ann Roripaugh

Milkweed Editions, Minneapolis. 2014: 98 pp.

Reviewed by Ryan Allen

Lee Ann Roripaugh is a translator – of language, space, trauma, loss, and rebirth. Her fourth poetry collection, *Dandarians* (2014), plays with language, meaning, identity, and the very nature of reality itself by asking, how does one reconcile being lost, where is there justice for the victim, and what happens when you can't find your voice? The speaker in these poems is trapped in the in-between spaces of language and meaning, bodies and self, and places where even breath is "taken hostage" (40). There are mispronunciations, misunderstandings, and mistaken identities. There's a poet mining the gaps, translating trauma, seeking the story within the story: her story versus his story, the mother's story in contrast to the daughter's, a Japanese story interweaving within an American one. *Dandarians* is an exploration of the mis- or unspoken spaces between absence and presence, loss and gain, perpetrator and victim, the places where "Dee Aster is always imminent" (59). So *Dandarians* is about fallout too – from family, from sexual violence, and from the societal ignorance and malaise that makes it impossible to reconcile trauma. What we have in this collection is a "word problem" where the victim is "forever marked" (94) and left to wonder how to behave or just be. The violin thief in Roripaugh's collection, the poet reminds us, "isn't boy or girl, man or woman, ghost or hallucination" (95): trauma is the thief, the perpetual taker (95). This collection is a public record of stolen property, and of the fight for who gets to claim authority – in our families, in society, and within ourselves.

From its outset, *Dandarians* takes us to another place, a "house of slippery signifiers and incongruities" (57), a realm where words and meanings, signs and maps can get confusing. On the planet of Dandar, "dandelions are *Dandarians*" (3), there's a "Secret Code," "everything garbles to Babel" (4), and it's up to a child to translate *senchimental*, *antimoaney*, and *feminint* as she oscillates between Hiroshima and Wyoming. There's an other-worldliness to it all until we remember we're on the banks of the Vermillion River in South Dakota or in eastern Wyoming and talking about an eight-year-old little girl being raped by a seventeen-year-old neighbor. "I am not confused" (79), the young girl asserts, even as the older speaker admits, "The things he does to me I have no name for yet" (78). In *Dandarians*, the gap in understanding isn't about the violence that happened, but rather in the ability to translate it, to speak and call it by its proper name.

In *Dandarians*, self-awareness is a crooked highway. "The more of an open wound I become, the more I try to hide" (80), the poet writes. She goes on to ask, "Is this brokenness a broken thing or a thing breaking open to let something else in?" (38). Can we gain from loss? Can we keep what is submerged underwater? Roripaugh writes, "my mother tells me I must never ever tell anyone what happened. She says girls are like submarines" (81). Yet, we see what comes out on the other side: self-mutilation, a "morbid obsess[ion] with amputation," shame, and a "terrible sense of impending doom" (79-80). Do bruises like this ever really heal? Where do they go as they return to the body? She's asking in "Bruised Interrogation." This trauma rarely is spoken outright. In "Trompe L'Oeil: The Annotated Version," the poet asks, "why do you always gather back up into yourself – when what you really want is to howl and screech and keen?" (15).

Roripaugh's *Dandarians* reminds us that trauma is circular – always passing, always beginning again. In "Griots' Signposts," she writes, "No matter where you go, it will not let you be" (12) and in "Annealing" she adds, "day by day you drink the memory of that blaze, that pear-rapture, that fall and bloom to icy water" (45).

And yet, at the suspension bridge in "Thirteen Ways of Looking at the Vermillion River," the poet recognizes the need to push back against the darkness.

In *Dandarians*, a mythological *I* emerges, not *Dee Aster*, but *Lee Aster*. Roripaugh writes, "it's just like me to protect myself from disaster by attempting to (re)write it(!) as a flower [. . .]" (59). Roripaugh's work reminds us that one does not simply *get over it* or *move on*. It's not a switch to be flipped. Trauma is real. Its impact is forever. *Dandarians*, though, lights a path: it's in speaking the trauma, translating the mispronunciations, and facing the evil and violence square in the face that the poet does her work. The poet's job is language. Making words, making meaning is the only defense. In "Antimacassar," she writes, "it's time to lift the veil. Try and read the writing on the sky" (28). In *Dandarians*, Lee Ann Roripaugh is coding survival, "HTMLing together a web to trap [her]self" (89). *Dandarians* shines where the world lives dark. The poet writes, "I am that strange glimmer" (25). We would all do well to pay attention to the light.

Running to the Fire: An American Missionary Comes of Age in Revolutionary Ethiopia, Tim Bascom

University of Iowa Press, Iowa City. 2015: 232 pp.

Reviewed by Tom Montag

The "last lap" device for ordering material in creative nonfiction – throwing the reader into the heat of a crisis which won't be resolved until near the end of the book – is somewhat predictable these days, but continues to be used because it so powerfully creates interest and tension and shows us what's at stake. We know right off in Tim Bascom's *Running to the Fire* what's at stake, and where, and who's in danger. It is the teenage Bascom and his missionary-doctor father, on a bus at 7,000 feet in the Ethiopian highlands, being confronted by a machine-gun-wielding Marxist revolutionary about their Christian faith.

> *"You are doctor, but you think Bible is good?"*
> *"Yes."*
> *Maybe, the younger Bascom thinks, "we shouldn't have come back to Ethiopia. Maybe we should have stayed in Kansas."*

One problem of the "last lap" story shape for first person creative nonfiction is that the reader already knows the protagonist has survived. Bascom also lets slip, before the resolution scene, that his father survived as well. So one particular crisis is not the whole of Bascom's story.

This is the story of a missionary family returning to Ethiopia during the Marxist revolution of the mid-70s, of the dangers they encountered, and the courage they exhibited. It is the story of a boy coming of age, of first love, and of love lost when the missionaries are evicted from the country. It is the story of Bascom's changing faith. It is, in part, the story of imperialist Christianity in Africa and of missionary Marxism in Ethiopia. And, finally, it is the story of the Ethiopian people coming to have the land which rightfully belongs to them.

It was back in Ethiopia that Bascom began to wrestle with his parents' Evangelical Protestantism. At one point in his narrative, I had to wonder whether the teen's killing of a dove with bow and arrow at the missionary compound in Addis Ababa might be a quiet metaphor for his rejection of his parents' missionary work. A decade later he would come to acknowledge "just how pharisaical we could be." And now he is an Episcopalian, practicing in a church "receptive to the life we lead as physical beings."

"Coming of age" is part of the story, although the angst and the intensity of those years may seem overblown to us now. It is the nature of adolescent hormones to make every joy the greatest joy and every loss inconsolable. After Bascom told his girlfriend, Nancy, goodbye for the final time, "I moved through each day in a kind of catatonic numbness, hardly aware of anything but my empty core. I never knew that a body could hold so much emptiness." Ah, young love. I miss it.

A subtheme about belonging and not belonging gives Bascom's story an added poignancy.

Perhaps the most subtle theme arching through *Running to the Fire* has to do with place, with "meaningful space," with claims to the land and local meanings assigned to place, and with missionaries "disregarding the notion that certain trees and hills were sacred sites where sacrifices should be offered." If you pay attention throughout, you won't be surprised by the final words of the book, spoken by a native Ethiopian whom Bascom met on a recent return trip: "Now we have our own land."

I like the idea of splitting the narrative voice in a memoir between who the author used to be and who the author is now. Such stereoscopic vision allows for authorial reflection which would not be possible if the narrator stayed within the character of his younger self. There's a danger, however, that the voices might mix, that the older, wiser self might speak for the younger persona, leading the reader to say "I don't think you actually thought that then." In some passages, the younger Bascom seems too wise. A minor quibble.

Another minor quibble. It is always good to paint detail into remembered scenes, but in Bascom's account of his teen years in Troy, Kansas, just before the family returned to Ethiopia, the mass of pop culture details amounts almost to special pleading. You want to say: "I believe you. I believe you."

Yet Bascom's telling throughout is always frank and honest in terms of his own life and that of his parents, and is almost brutal in its truth when considering the misadventures of both Christians and Marxists in Ethiopia. This is not the slide show a returning missionary would give us in the church basement on Wednesday evening. Bascom's story won't recruit any missionaries. The telling is not bitter, but true, is clear-eyed, lyrical. I admire that.

So how does that crisis on the bus with the Marxist soldiers come to conclusion? This way:

> *"I am letting you go," the officer finally said, "but only because doctor. And I am letting this one go. Is he your son?"*
> *"Yes."*
> *"I am letting him go only because you are doctor."*
> *Then he handed the Bible back to Dad as if it smelled bad.*

The Collector of Names, Patrick Hicks

Schaffner Press, Tucson. 2015: 200 pp.

Reviewed by Matthew Pangborn

The characters in Patrick Hicks' new short-story collection, *The Collector of Names* (Schaffner Press, 2015), all inhabit a Minnesota of "snow and thunderstorms," of the smells and sounds of Catholic Mass, and of the closeness of small prairie towns (198). What they also share, however, is the near presence of a death that is brutal, sudden, inexplicable – but also, at times, capable of something almost like magic.

In the first story, "57 Gatwick," death's magic is of the decidedly spectacular variety. A County Coroner roams Duluth after a mid-air explosion has ripped through a passenger jet 29,000 feet above the city. George, who has recently lost his own wife, staggers, dazed, from one corpse to another: "a man belted into his seat holding a book," a "baby … in a tree" (4). George feels some sense of responsibility for these victims, some urge to act, but what can he do in the face of this overwhelming tragedy?

The same need for response is felt by characters confronted with deaths much more mundane. In "Living with the Dead," two high school biology lab partners dissect a frog. One is a girl whose mother is being treated for breast cancer at the Mayo Clinic; the other is an undertaker's son. And the response of the boy is representative of so many of the human beings who inhabit Hicks' stories, all good people, all struggling to understand:

> *"This poor thing was alive one minute, doing his froggy thing, and then … then he's in a tray with his stomach ripped open." Her bottom eyelashes beaded with tears and her voice filled with fire. "It's not fair. People shouldn't have to die. They shouldn't."*
>
> *For some reason I nudged her elbow. "The end of life makes us appreciate the journey more. If we lived forever we'd take everything for granted, don't you think? The world only looks beautiful because we know someday we won't be in it anymore. End of life makes us love life. Don't you think?"*
>
> *She looked at me for a long moment and then smiled. "Would you like to see a movie with me?"*
>
> *I nodded because I'd never been asked out by a girl before.* (16–17)

In such a way does death prompt something just as important in those who are confronted by it. The lifeless body of a frog, the slow "gobbling up" of a mother by cancer, the dying that feeds a family business: all contribute to the making of new connections, of new life (18).

In "The Chemical Equation of Loss," one of two stories in the collection originally published in *The Briar Cliff Review,* this theme is made explicit when a young woman, reflecting on memories of her dead chemist father, recalls his words to her that "we only borrow atoms. They're never ours to keep" (128). Atoms from a corpse go on to join others in a new body. Life is always moving, always creating. And the only adequate human responses to these truths is to pay our own respects and remember – to create, ourselves.

The bullied fourth grader of the title story, the other of the book's tales that originally appeared in this magazine, is thus not the only character to find surprising ways of memorializing those who have been lost. Nerdy Keegan McCabe decides, in response to an assignment given to him by Sister Herbert, to write a paragraph about each person he has ever met in his life, a project that comes to span four decades and have an unexpected end. But Keegan is of course only the representative of the author himself, who wants to bring to the reader's attention all of the life flickering past us every day, that which we might not notice, never mind fully appreciate and honor, in our distraction and inattention. And the chemist father's "atoms" are only stand-ins for those elements that really compose a human life, which are stories. As another character searching after a memory of a junior high classmate realizes:

> *I suppose we're all reduced to anecdotes in the end. The meat of our lives is shaved into thin slices and served up for conversation. All the sunrises we've seen, the peanut butter sandwiches we've eaten, the lips we've kissed, the shoes we've bought, all the crappy jobs we've held, all the tears and underhanded deeds and acts of generosity and Christmas presents and toothaches and music and laughter and hugs, it all gets buried. In the end we're reduced to stories that are told to other people. Our lives are never really our own.* (37)

Hicks' own skill as a writer ensures that no one who appears in his stories is ever "reduced." Full of vitality and doubts, capable as much of making mistakes as making vital meaning, his characters grapple with the hardest question of our lives. And they do so in moments that will stick with the reader long after. Throughout this wonderful collection, then, if Hicks guides us to discover in these shared moments, not consumption and loss, but inspiration and generosity, he does so with a magic to more than match even death's own.

Flavian Mark Lupinetti

Excalibur

Now, in the hour of my greatest crisis,
I remember my grandfather,
and I recall a day when he
planted his peppers, tamping down
the dirt around each tiny plant.
When he finished, he set up his folding chair,
the one with interlaced ribbons of green and white
plastic webbing, frayed at the edges
and stretched out in the middle of the seat
by decades of use.
His shovel rested across his lap,
the shovel he once used to load coal out of
Green Creek Mine Number Eight.
Thirty something years he wielded
that shovel, that shovel he now
gripped in his blue-veined hands,
his forearms steady as the pillars of slate
that keep the earth from collapsing onto
a miner's head.
He tapped me with that shovel,
first on one shoulder, then on
the other, the way a king
touches a knight with his sword.
If I had that shovel today,
I swear, I could dig my way out.

Sedative

Bronson L. Wilson
spray paint on canvas

Contributors

Kate Bullard Adams, Charleston, SC, has published in *Chautauqua, Harpur Palate,* and *Portland Review.* She is working on a novel, *Bailout.*

Bob Allen, Phoenix, AZ, is retired after forty years as an administrator in government, colleges, universities, and the arts. His art has been displayed throughout the US and is in private collections in California, New York, Illinois, Indiana, Kentucky, among others.

Ryan Allen, Sioux City, IA, is an associate professor of English and writing at BCU. His work has appeared in *Under the Sun, The Louisville Review, South Dakota Review, A Prairie Journal,* and others.

Michael Anania, Austin, TX, is the author of numerous books, his most recent including *In Natural Light* and *Heat Lines. Continuous Showings,* a collection of poetry, will be published in 2016.

Christopher Todd Anderson, Pittsburg, KS, is an associate professor of English at Pittsburg State University in Kansas. His poetry has appeared in *Tar River Poetry, River Styx,* and *Chicago Quarterly Review,* among others.

Laura Apol, Lyons, MI, is an associate professor at Michigan State University. She has three poetry collections as well as numerous publications. She has been awarded the ArtPrize, the Golden Quill, Pat Schneider awards for poetry, and Leaf Press international competition for her chapbook, *Celestial Bodies.*

Linda Bagshaw, Sioux City, IA, teaches writing at a local community college and has published several poetry collections.

Lisa Beans, Sioux City, IA, received her MFA from West Virginia University and taught on a Fulbright Scholarship in Krakow, Poland. Her poems have appeared in *Raleigh Review, The Southeast Review, Barnstorm,* and others.

John Beckelman, Cedar Rapids, IA, is an art professor at Coe College. His works have recently been exhibited in the *4th Central Time Ceramics Exhibition.*

Nancy Lael Braun, Lone Tree, IA, works as an organizational development consultant. Her poems have been published in *Barbaric Yawp, Iowa City: Poetry in Public Poetalk, Small Brushes,* and *The Southampton Review,* among others.

Jesse Breite, Atlanta, GA, has had poetry appear in *Tar River Poetry, Chiron Review,* and *Prairie Schooner,* among others. His first chapbook, *The Knife Collector,* was published in 2013.

Gaylord Brewer, Murfreesboro, TN, teaches at Middle Tennessee State University. His most recent books are *Country of Ghost* and *The Poet's Guide to Food, Drink, and Desire.*

Jack Bristow, Sioux City, IA, has been in the Sioux City Camera Club since retiring from Siouxland OB/Gyn. Photography has been his hobby since age ten.

Corey Broman, Omaha, NE, works in a glass studio he built himself. He studied at Hastings College. He has shown his work privately and in several galleries mainly in the Midwest and on the west coast. He is represented by Gallery 72, Omaha, NE.

Jenny Bye, Sioux Falls, SD, is an encaustic artist and has had works exhibited at the Sioux City Art Center, The Washington Pavilion, and Eastbank Art Gallery.

William Cass, San Diego, CA, has published over eighty short stories in magazines like *december* and won *The Examined Life Journal's* writing contest.

Lucia Cherciu, Poughkeepsie, NY, is a professor of English at SUNY/Dutchess Community College. Her poetry has been nominated twice for a Pushcart Prize and Best of the Net.

Karen Chesterman, Sioux City, IA, holds an MFA in painting from USD and has had many exhibitions. She holds Best in Show awards and several Special Recognition in Painting awards.

Rob Cook, New York City, NY, is the author of six collections, including *Undermining of the Democratic Club, Blueprints for a Genocide,* and *Empire in the Shake of a Grass Blade.* His work has appeared in *Asheville Poetry Review, Tampa Review, Minnesota Review, Harvard Review, Colorado Review,* and others.

Brian Damon, McCook Lake, SD, is a BCU art graduate. He has had works exhibited at the DeWitt Theater in Orange City, IA, and the Washington Pavilion in Sioux Falls, SD.

Laura S. Distelheim, Highland Park, IL, has appeared in numerous journals and anthologies, has been noted for special mention in Best American Essays and the Pushcart Prize, and has received the Mary Roberts Rinehart Award, the Richard J. Margolis Award, an Illinois Arts Council Fellowship Award, a Barbara Deming Memorial Fund Grant, and the William Faulkner-William Wisdom Medal.

Barbara Duffey, Mitchell, SD, is a NEA Literature Fellow in poetry and has won the Washington Prize from The Word Works. She is an assistant professor of English at Dakota Wesleyan University.

Elaine Erickson, Urbandale, IA, has published in *Midwest Poetry Review* and *Maryland Poetry Review.* She is the author of four collections and three chapbooks, her latest being *New Portraits.*

David Evans, Sioux City, IA, is the author of nine collections of poetry; his most recent is *The Carnival, The Life.* A Fulbright scholar to China twice, he has received several writing grants, as well as the 2009 South Dakota Governor's Award for Distinction for Creative Achievement. He served as Poet Laureate of SD from 2002-2015.

Patricia Fargnoli, Walpole, NH, is the author of seven collections of poetry. She has won several awards and has recently been published in *Prairie Schooner, Paterson Literary Review,* and *Alaska Quarterly Review,* among others.

Luiza Flynn-Goodlett, San Francisco, CA, is the author of the chapbook *Congress of Mud.* She received her MFA from The New School and has been awarded the Andrea Klein Willison Prize for Poetry. Her work has been in numerous literary journals, including *The Greensboro Review* and *The Missouri Review Online.*

Michael Frizzell, Sioux City, IA, is an art and education major at BCU.

Contributors

Robert Gillespie, Sioux City, IA, is a landscape photographer. His recent galleries include Betty Strong Encounter Center, Sioux City Art Center, and Dahl Art Center. He also has four pictures selected for the 2016 Pinnacle Bank Calendar.

Rachel Ann Girty, Evanston, IL, is a writer and a classical singer. She works as a poetry editor of Helicon magazine. Her work has appeared in *An Artprize Anthology, Perfume River Poetry Review*, and *Sixfold Magazine*, among others.

Twyla M. Hansen, Lincoln, NE, has six books of poetry and was a finalist for the WILLA Literary High Plains Book Award. Her writing has appeared in Prairie Schooner, Midwest Quarterly, South Dakota Review, and Crazy Woman Creek: Woman Rewrite the American West, among others.

Kathleen Hellen, Baltimore, MD, is a poet, educator, and former journalist. She is the author of the award-winning collection *Umberto's Night* and two chapbooks, *The Girl Who Loved Mothra* and *Pentimento*.

Joyce Hinnefeld, Bethlehem, PA, is a professor of English at Moravian College where she directed the Moravian Writers' Conference in 2014 and 2015. She is the author of a short story collection and two novels.

Rick Johns, Vermillion, SD, is an artist whose abstracts explore the nature of paint and the surprise and beauty discovered in the process.

Ron Johns, Spink, SD, has been a freelance photographer for over 25 years. His photography can be found in *Photographer's Forum, Gourmet*, and *National Geographic Traveler*.

William Jolliff, Portland, OR, is an English professor at George Fox University. His writing has appeared in *Southern Poetry Review, Midwest Quarterly, Appalachian Journal, Poet Lore*, and other journals. His most recent published collection is *Twisted Shapes of Light*.

Steve Joy, Omaha, NE, was born in Plymouth, England, and has exhibited in galleries in Spain, France, Norway, Switzerland, and the US.

Jacqueline Kluver, Omaha, NE, received her BFA from UNO. She is a full-time painter and has participated in numerous solo and group exhibitions. She is represented by Modern Arts Midtown, Omaha, NE.

Mark Kochen, Sioux City, IA, is a full-time artist.

Greg Kosmicki, Omaha, NE, is the founder and Emeritus editor of *The Backwaters Press*. He is the author of four collections and seven chapbooks of poetry. He works with his wife in the social work field.

Rustin Larson, Fairfield, IA, has appeared in *The New Yorker, The Iowa Review, North American Review*, and *Poetry East*, among others. He is the author of several works and was the winner of the 2013 Blue Light Book Award.

Mercedes Lawry, Seattle, WA, has been published in *Poetry, Natural Bridge, Nimrod*, and *Prairie Schooner*. She has received honors from the Seattle Arts Commission, Artist Trust, Richard Hugo House, and has been nominated for the Pushcart Prize three times.

Jenna Le, Minneapolis, MN, is the author of Six Rivers, a Small Press Distribution Bestseller, and a *History of the Cetacean American Diaspora*. Her poetry, fiction, essays, criticism, and translations appear or are forthcoming in *AGNI Online, The Los Angeles Review, Massachusetts Review, The Village Voice*, and elsewhere.

Nancy Losacker, Vermillion, SD, has exhibited her work throughout the US and Europe. She teaches art and other classes for Vermillion's public schools and for Vermillion Area Arts Council. She began collaborating with Norma Wilson in 2008.

Flavian Mark Lupinetti, Orono, ME, has stories and poems appearing in *Barrelhouse, Bellevue Literary Review, Cutthroat, Neon*, and *Red Rock Review*, among others. He practices cardiac surgery.

S.J. MacLean, Donville, CA, has been published in I*nkwell, Pennsylvania Literary Review*, and *May Day Magazine*. She is working on a cycle of stories and a novel.

Louise Marburg, New York City, NY, has been published in *Cold Mountain Review, Reed*, and *The Louisville Review*. She is an MFA graduate of Columbia University's School of the Arts.

Sadie Martin, Sioux City, IA, is an art/criminal justice major at BCU.

Alyssa Mazzarella, Roslindale, MA, has appeared in *apt, Common Ground Review*, and *Freshwater*. She was a semifinalist for a Provincetown Fine Arts Work Center Writing Fellowship. She currently works as an adjunct professor and tutor at the University of Massachusetts in Boston.

M.B. McLatchey, New Smyrna Beach, FL, is the author of a poetry collection, *Advantages of Believing*, which was awarded the 2014 FLP Chapbook Prize by Finishing Line Press. She is currently Poet Laureate of Volusia County, FL, and associate professor of Humanities at Embry-Riddle Aeronautical University in Daytona Beach.

Ann Marie McTaggart, Sioux City, IA, was an oncology RN before she received a degree in studio art from Morningside as well as a BFA and MA from USD. Her work has been on display throughout the Midwest and New York, along with several solo shows.

Angelica A. Mercado, Fremont, NE, is an art and writing major at BCU.

Christopher A. Meyer, Vermillion, SD, has had solo exhibits in the Norstrand Gallery at Wayne State College, at BCU's Clausen Art Gallery, and the Norfolk Arts Center. He teaches sculpture at USD.

Tom Montag, Fairwater, WI, is a poet, essayist, and author of *Curlew: Home, The Idea of the Local, Middle Ground, The Big Book of Ben Zen*, and *In This Place*. He was the featured poet in Atticus Review in April 2015 and received two Pushcart Prize nominations in 2015 as well.

Michael S. Moos, St. Paul, MN, is the author of *A Long Way to See, Morning Windows*, and *Hawk Hover*. He has received NEA and Loft-McKnight awards and won MN Voices. He has an MFA from Columbia University.

Contributors

Matthew Pangborn, Sioux City, IA, is chair and assistant professor of the Modern Languages Department at BCU and co-editor of fiction for *The Briar Cliff Review*. He has published on eighteenth-and nineteenth-century American literature, film, television, and literary theory.

Benjamin Pratt, Sioux City, IA, is a 2011 BCU art graduate and is currently a practicing artist at his studio in the Benson Building.

Thomas Prinz, Omaha, NE, has been featured in several galleries, including Modern Arts Midtown and Creighton University. He is represented by Anderson O'Brien Fine Art, Omaha, NE.

Richard Robbins, Mankato, MN, has been featured in *Cincinnati Review, Hubbub*, and *Indiana Review*. His fourth and fifth poetry books, *Radioactive City* and *Other Americas*, were published recently. He was a fellow at the Hawthornden Castle International Retreat for Writers in Scotland.

Larry Roots, Omaha, NE, is a painter and sculptor who has exhibited extensively including shows at the University of Northern Colorado, the Museum of Nebraska Art, the Sheldon Museum, and the Sioux City Art Center. His work is represented by Modern Arts Midtown, Omaha, where he serves as a director.

Barbara Saunier, Marnie, MI, has received two Pushcart Prize nominations, and has won first place in the Poetry Society of Michigan's *Peninsula Poets*. She has also been published in *Parting Gifts, Dunes Review*, and *Big Scream*.

Christina Seymour, Maryville, TN, has had her poetry and essays featured in *North American Review, Cimarron Review, New Haven Review, Wick Poetry Center's Exhibit, Speak Peace – American Voices Respond to Vietnamese Children's Paintings*, and elsewhere. She teaches creative writing at Maryville College in Tennessee.

Liv Spikes, Erie, CO, has published in *The Kokanee* and dozens of spiral-bound journals. She is currently working on a full-length memoir in Erie, where she lives with her husband and two children.

Jacqueline Sullivan, Arlington, MA, is a Phi Beta Kappa graduate of the College of the Holy Cross. She is an attorney and was a Joshua A. Guberman Teaching Fellow at Brandeis University. Her poetry has been recently published in *Cold Mountain Review*.

Z.G. Tomaszewski, Grand Rapids, MI, was awarded the 2014 International Poetry Prize for his first book *All Things Dusk* and was published by Hong Kong University Press. New poems will appear in *The Cortland Review, Midwestern Gothic*, and *The 3288 Review*, among others.

Dennis Trudell, Madison, WI, has recently been nominated for the Pushcart Prize. His book, *Fragments in Us: Recent & Earlier Poems*, was published by University of Wisconsin Press. He also edited *Full Court: A Literary Anthology of Basketball*.

Pat Underwood, Colfax, IA, is a Pushcart Prize nominee and the author of *Gatherings, The Last Supper*, and *At Coloring Zoo*. She has received the Founder's Award twice from the National Federation of State Poetry Societies. She is a contributor to *Voices on the Landscape: Contemporary Iowa Poets* and has appeared in numerous journals.

Willie VerSteeg, Columbus, OH, is a San Diego native whose poetry and criticism appear in *The Kenyon Review, The Southern Humanities Review, Tar River Poetry, BOAAT Journal*, and elsewhere.

Jesse Wallis, Glendale, AZ, has been published in *New Ohio Review, Poet Lore, Poetry East, Rhino, The Southern Review*, and *Zone 3*, among others. He studied at the University of Iowa, Syracuse University, and California Institute of Arts.

Michael Walsh, Sioux City, IA, is a Senior District Court Judge. He has had his photographs on display in The Sioux City Art Center and The Lewis and Clark Interpretive Center, and published in *The Briar Cliff Review* and the *Iowa State Fair Photography Salon Book*.

Graceann Warn, Ann Arbor, MI, is a full-time artist, and has been exhibited internationally. She is in collections at Yale University, US Embassies in Nairobi and Sarajevo, Pew Charitable Trust, and many others. She is represented by Modern Arts Midtown, Omaha, NE.

David Watts, San Francisco, CA, is the author of two collections of short stories and seven books of poetry. He has just released his newest book, *The Lucifer Connection*, a San Francisco mystery novel.

Karen J. Weyant, Jamestown, NY, teaches at Jamestown Community College. She has poetry and prose published in *Harpur Palate, Slipstream, Tahoma Literary Review*, and *River Styx*. She has published two chapbooks.

David L. White, Tempe, AZ, is a creative writing instructor. He has previously appeared in *THRUSH Poetry Journal, Salamander, Paper Nautilus, Potomac Review*, and *PRISM international*.

Jodi Whitlock, Sioux City, IA, has recently exhibited her work at Vangarde Arts. She is an adjunct faculty member at Morningside College and WITCC.

Randall D. Williams, Sioux City, IA, is a medical technologist. His images have been published in *The Briar Cliff Review*.

Bronson L. Wilson, Council Bluffs, IA, is a history and secondary education major at BCU.

Norma Wilson, Vermillion, SD, is an English Professor Emeritus at USD. Her books include *The Nature of Native American Poetry* and *Under the Rainbow: Poems from Mojácar*. She began collaborating with Nancy Losacker in 2008.

Lucas Woolfolk, Sioux City, IA, is an art and psychology major at BCU.